Dearest Darling,
120 balloons would not fit in your car but that is what I wanted to buy.
Happy Anniversary
With all my love
Kai

CARRY
AIRPLANE
Till the honeymoon continues
How I love you
Kai

Just because
all my Love
Kai

My Dearest — 3/10/85
You are my "magic man,"
my precious dear one,
my greatest lover,
my best friend,
my laughing companion,
my pal in mischief,
my partner in inspiration,
my tender toucher
my imaginative imp,
my romantic husband
my self-sacrificing love,
my strong protector
my powerful provider,

my intellectual conspirator,
my provocateur,
my partner in luxury,
my first class man,
my comforter
my joy,
my soul,
my heart,
my past
And my future.
I love you.
Hurry to me.

I love you more than all the Delegates multiplied by all the Grains of Sand on the beaches in California.
You look wonderful and are doing beautifully. I am so proud of you.
your loving Husband —
"Sudi"

Guess Who?

DARLING ~
TO MAKE
THIS DAY
BETTER!
Love
Kai

A Passion for Living

By Danuta Soderman

Dear Danuta

A Passion for Living

A Passion for Living

DANUTA

Fleming H. Revell Company
Old Tappan, New Jersey

Scripture quotations are from the King James Version of the Bible.

ISBN 1-8007-1534-9

Published by the Fleming H. Revell Company
Old Tappan, New Jersey 07675
Printed in the United States of America

*T*his book is dedicated to
Johnny,
Peter, Paul, Sally,
Jennifer, Polly, Robin, and Michelle.

Remember ye not the former things, neither consider the things of old. Behold, I will do a new thing; now it shall spring forth; shall ye not know it? I will even make a way in the wilderness, and rivers in the desert.

Isaiah 43:18, 19

Contents

Passion

excitement
flush
heat
fever
fire
flame
fume
tumult
effervescence
ebullition
gust
storm
tempest
burst
fit
explosion
outbreak
scene
outburst
agony
fullness of the heart

A Passion
for Living

Chapter One
Endings and Beginnings

Kai's Story
October 1973

*T*he end had come in the soft thud of a closing door. It had the eerie voice of finality with a presence that nearly lived, startling the morning air, sending a shudder through the empty parking lot.

The white Cadillac sat like a shimmering tombstone against the stark asphalt, dominating the natural surroundings of a wooded park.

The man in the eight-hundred-dollar suit gripped a ninety-eight-cent piece of rope and walked into the forest to find a suitable tree to hang himself.

The narrow paths of the tree preserve were beaten down to exposed tree roots and jagged rocks. The underbrush grabbed at his pant legs as he made his way toward the heart of the woods, crossing over the footpath to a more obscure setting. He wanted to be hidden from possible passersby. He scanned the trees, looking for a branch that would take his weight. One promising branch snapped off in his hands. But then he saw what he was looking for: growing at a nearly ninety-degree angle from the trunk, a strong limb jutted out at him from an old pine tree.

The world stood still as the man and the limb confronted each other, each waiting for the other to make the first move. Trying to gulp down some air and force the sickening feeling from his throat, Kai Soderman wrapped his arms around the tree. Scraping at the bark with his newly shined shoes, he managed to wrestle up to the first beckoning branch and sit, awkwardly straddling the limb, shirttail out, suit rumpled, a wet blemish darkening the back of his jacket where shoulders pressed against a shirt sticking with perspiration from the effort and the anguish.

A long, low moan came from somewhere inside of him, exploding into uncontrolled sobs at his feeble attempts to carry out his execution with dignity. Purged and exhausted, he leaned his back against the trunk, closed his eyes, and ran through his life, looking for something to hold onto.

Scenes from a personal sideshow blazed in his brain. A big house in Princeton, New Jersey. A city council member proclaiming him "a pillar of the community." Rumors that he could run for the council, or for mayor, maybe even Congress. He was one of the top twenty-five insurance salesmen in the country, a sought-after speaker for the Million Dollar Round Table. The father of six. The husband of a recovering alcoholic in a loveless marriage. The big-spending provider for a meaningless existence, needing more to life and finding less and less worth living for. He was gripped by depression and by the prescribed medications that only numbed his senses but couldn't reach the pain.

He had been drowning for years. There was no escape, no hope, only an endless battle with duty.

But there were the kids, and his wife, and he had provided for them in his life insurance and in his will. In his troubled mind, he convinced himself they were better off without him. He was a man possessed by a need that he could not name and so could not find.

The final blow had come at the dinner table, when his wife of seventeen years announced, "I don't need to be married to you." The provider was better off dead. Too much work, too much pressure, too many days on top of other days, trapped by an image, a myth parading as a man. He saw no way out.

He opened his eyes and somberly slung one end of the rope around the limb and fashioned a Boy Scout knot to anchor the rope to the branch. With the other end, he tied a hoop with a slipknot, pulled it over his head, and twisted it around his neck.

One last time, he would close his eyes . . . and he remembered Johnny, his oldest son. "Dad, I just wanted you to know that, even though you and Mom are separated, I still need you to be my father. I love you, Dad."

Inhaling as if to block out the memory, he heard Johnny's words again: "I still need you to be my father."

It was over. "I can't help you, Johnny," he sobbed. He couldn't even help himself. Kai maneuvered his legs into a crouch position and readied himself to spring into oblivion.

Just then, voices. Dead ahead, two women were walking directly toward him, chattering like two early-spring robins. They were bird-watchers, searching the treetops looking for exotic breeds.

Shame flooded over him like warm red paint. Suddenly he saw himself: hunched over a tree limb like some bulky bird swollen to rumpled proportions, with a rope around its scraggly neck. The sense of impropriety burst upon him in this comedic vision of what the two bird-watchers would see if they should glance up to his tree. He made himself skinny and pressed against the tree without breathing. The bird-watchers passed below without seeing. The agony had passed above them. The moment was lost. He slid down the tree and drove back to his office, filled with overwhelming sadness.

Two hours later Kai Soderman admitted himself into a hospital. He called his family and nobody came.

Danuta's Story
April 1973

I was attending the University of Colorado, walking across campus with my arms loaded with books for my next class. I was a teacher's assistant in graduate school, and I had the dual responsibility of grading and sometimes lecturing undergraduate classes in communication. In addition, I was studying for my own classes toward a master's degree in communication. I was in a hurry. I was always in a hurry. Life never allowed me time to catch up to it. It was a passion, for I had to do everything, try everything, experience everything to the fullest.

I stepped over a small irrigation ditch on the campus grounds, and then my world faded to black.

I woke up two hours later, with my books scattered about me on the lawn. I had passed out. That never happened to me before. I jumped up, scooping my books to my chest, clutching at them for comfort. I looked around to see if anyone was watching me.

There was no one about. No one had seen me fall. No one had seen me at all. I brushed my hair back with my hand and hurried off.

There was no one to talk to about this, no one waiting for me at home. There had been no one for a long time.

A week later I blacked out again, so I paid a visit to the school's health clinic. A thorough checkup by the school doctor proclaimed me healthy as a horse. Blood count normal. Temperature normal. Blood pressure normal.

"Would you do me a favor?" the doctor asked me. "Would you talk with someone downstairs, and let's get to the bottom of this?"

Downstairs. That meant the school psychologist. He wanted me to talk to a shrink! Did he think I only *thought* I passed out? Did he think I was making this up?

"How have you been feeling lately?" the psychologist asked me.

"Well, doctor, I've been feeling just fine. I really don't know what the problem is."

"Let's look at it for a bit," he said. "Are you worried about money? Is that a big concern for you?"

"Money? Me?" I laughed. "Doctor, I have never had money, my parents have never had money—why should I worry about not having it now!"

"All right, if it's not money, what about grades? Are you worried about graduation?"

"No. I'm always on the dean's list. I make good grades. School's going fine."

"How about home? Any problems there?"

"Nope."

"Boyfriend trouble?"

I forced a laugh. "Now you really are reaching, doctor. I haven't got a boyfriend. Haven't got time for a boyfriend. Haven't for a long time. . . ."

"Do you have any friends you talk to when you just need someone to talk with?"

"No, not really. I haven't had time for friends. I'm carrying eighteen units in grad school. I'm a teacher's assistant. I have office hours, papers to grade—I don't have time for friends. But that's not the problem, doctor. I just can't seem to get my hair clean. It stays greasy all the time, my complexion is gray, I've passed out twice on campus. . . ."

"How long have you been feeling like this?" the doctor probed.

"About two weeks," I mumbled.

"And what do you do when you need someone to talk to?"

"Oh, I just write poetry, I guess."

"And how many poems have you written in the last two weeks?"

"I've written two poems. One last week, another this week." I didn't understand what he was getting at.

"Would you mind sharing them with me?" he asked with a smile.

"No, not at all. In fact, I think I can even remember them," I said, feeling a bit embarrassed at revealing myself with a spontaneous recitation. I wiggled in my chair, stared at a spot on the floor to remember the first poem, and began:

> Everything looked hard today . . .
> The gray and dreary clouds cloaked the city
> Like a dirty sheet . . .
> A stupid, muggy day without the energy to rain.
> I saw a small dog lying dead in the middle of the road—
> An ominous day—as if I were to die today.
> How vain! To think the whole world

Should cloud on my day of death!
As if everyone were to mourn my passing . . .
There are far brighter stars in the eyes of God
Who die without a whimper from this heartless world.
It was just another day alone,
And without love.

"Not very good, is it?" I said self-consciously.

"Oh, I don't know," the doctor said, leaning back in his chair, his hands folded in his lap. "I think it says a lot about you and how you're feeling, don't you?"

"I just write the poems, I don't try to analyze them," I said.

"If you will allow me, I'd like to try," he said. "But first, I'd like to hear the second one."

I wasn't sure I liked this. In fact, I didn't like this at all. I wasn't seeing any connection. But nonetheless, I cleared my throat and began again:

"This one is entitled 'Lost,' " I said, almost apologetically.

Charge your fires, hidden seeds of life!
I'm in search of Spring
And I am lost.
Eternal tree, perennial leaf,
You know what you are.
You are a tree, and you a leaf,
And I, no greater, nor lesser than that,
But only lost.
I seek you out, in a most holy unison
Of spirit and mind.
That I be you and you, me.
Most holy eternal tree, perennial leaf.
Then you shall know me,
By my patterned steps,
Sinking in April soil,
To a journey below your roots

To entangle me and draw me up
—A perennial leaf,
In search of Spring.

I looked up at the doctor, hoping I had not made a complete fool of myself. He was smiling at me. "That's very good," he said. "Do you hear what you are saying in those poems of yours?"

"I'm not sure what you're getting at."

"In one poem you are looking at the world in gray, dreary tones because you are feeling gray and dreary, and why? You said it yourself: because you have no one to love. That, my girl, is depression. And now look at the second poem. You are talking to a tree, asking the tree to take you in, to entangle you and draw you up, in, what did you say, a most holy union? Everywhere you look, there is springtime, Danuta. This is April. People fall in love, new growth is all around, but not for you. Your poems tell me that you are lonely; you are working too hard to take time to smell the roses. You have no friends, and most of all, you are not in love at a time when love is all around you. In short, you are lost. You even said it yourself."

"You were able to find all that in my poetry?"

"And more. My best advice to you is to read what you write. It could be your best therapy." He was smiling again.

"You mean, that's all it is? I'm just lonely and it's spring, so I'm depressed?"

"You've obviously had some pain in your life, but for now, I think you just need to slow down and enjoy yourself a little bit. And oh, yes, remember—your poetry is a window to yourself. Learn to use it."

I jumped up from the chair, feeling better already. I rushed home and took a bath and washed my hair. For the first time in weeks, I felt good about myself. At least now I knew what the problem was: I was lonely. I would never again allow it to get the better of me.

January 1976

I couldn't seem to get my hair clean. I washed it two and three times a day, but it still turned out oily and limp and utterly lifeless. My complexion didn't look any better. It was the color of a rainy day, gray and blotchy. I wasn't getting anywhere, and rejection was becoming my daily fare. Discouragement had set in, and my body responded to my attitude. I felt defeated. Job hunting in San Francisco was no piece of cake, especially in radio and television. Competition was tough enough as it was with seasoned professionals, even worse for a rookie looking for a break in the business.

I plastered the town with my brief and somewhat ineffectual resume: Anchorage, Alaska, high school student who became the Dick Clark of Anchorage as a dance show host every Saturday afternoon on local TV. University of Colorado, graduate in radio/TV/communication. Graduate student studying journalism, communication and philosophy. Teacher's assistant in grad school and graduate manager in charge of university television station. First female studio camera operator in Phoenix, Arizona, with occasional stints as news reporter. There was a smattering of odds and ends such as consultant to the "Candid Camera" show with Allen Funt for a few months, owner and operator of a swim school for infants, and part-time cocktail waitress to help make ends meet. Not very impressive.

After walking the streets of the city and knocking on every

media door in town with no success, I turned around and started over again, hoping someone had changed his mind, or else died, giving me another chance to overwhelm an executive with my enthusiasm if not my expertise. I was willing to accept any position—overnight disc jockey, sound grip, newswriter, floor sweeper, anything except secretary. I felt that once I became a secretary, I'd always be labeled a secretary and permanently overlooked for any serious broadcast job.

Job hunting seemed a long way from my days at the University of Colorado. Just a few years earlier I was hurling my body, at forty-five miles an hour, down a ski slope, at night, toward disaster.

I had been skiing ever since my father made my first pair of skis when I was only three years old. Dad had been an Olympic skier for Poland, and in the winter months, he was a ski pro at the local ski resorts in both Canada and Michigan. I grew to love the sport as much as he did. I chose to go to the University of Colorado, to ski as much as to study.

Night skiing had always been a fascination for me. The snow glows blue in the moonlight, and turns to silk under the little puddles of man-made light.

I had just won the giant slalom event in an intramural ski race, and I wanted to take a victory run. I cruised out behind the ski lift, looking for the perfect isolated slope where I could carve my tracks in the snow. I was alone. I was deliciously alone. I could hear my heartbeat in the nocturnal silence of the mountains. The snow was twinkling at me like a Christmas card.

I approached the edge of an advanced slope where no one had marked the snow. I would be the first. The slope was an endless checkerboard of blue moonlight and white silk puddles. I shoved off with my poles and slipped into heaven, soundlessly flying through powder. Five inches of new snow cushioned a deep, fast base, and I quickly picked up speed, but all my senses kept me in luxurious slow motion.

Snow powder floated into my face and billowed behind me into trails of snow and air.

My skis seemed part of me, responding to every thought, every flex of muscle and shift in weight, and I was a part of the mountain, the snow, the cold stars. We were singing the same jubilant, passionate song: This was liberty! This was freedom! Flying, flying through space and time. This was truth and mystery, the authenticity of life itself, all wrapped up into one harmonious moment of exquisite living! And then pain. The edges of my skis sparked like flint against steel. I collided with a pile of rocks, disguised as a mound of snow.

The ski patrol found me on the last of their rounds, on my stomach. I was screaming, one ski tilted up behind me, stuck in the snow up to my boot, my kneecap crushed into bedrock, my hand bent back from the knuckles.

By toboggan and then by ambulance I was rushed to the school clinic, two hours away. By the time the doctor got to me, the pain was so intense, he had to cut my ski pants off with a pair of scissors, trying not to move me.

The diagnosis was grim. I had torn ligaments and tendons in and around my left knee, pulling the knee out of its socket, and broken my right hand.

A cast was set from the base of my left foot to the top of my thigh, and another cast from above my right elbow to the middle of my hand, with a splint holding up the middle finger. The prognosis: I would never ski again, one leg would be several inches shorter than the other, and the casts would have to stay in place for at least six weeks.

I was carried home wrapped in a bed sheet, put to bed, and left alone.

It was three o'clock in the morning and I had to go to the bathroom. I had crutches, but with a broken right hand and left leg, the use of crutches was impossible. I was completely immobilized. That's when the panic set in. I was in pain. The casts were heavy and uncomfortable. I started shaking uncontrollably. I was alone. I still didn't have a friend in the world. I had been too busy trying to survive. But I had been following doctor's orders, writing and reading my poetry!

I lay in that bed in shock. "What am I going to do? I can't walk. I can't even crawl."

There was only one thing left to do. I would call the strongest, tallest man I knew. His name was J.J. He was one of my undergraduate students in my Communication 101 class. He was always so cheerful, and he seemed to make friends with everyone he met. I felt I could trust him, so I called him.

"Hello, J.J.?"

"Yes . . ." replied a groggy, sleepy voice.

"J.J., this is Danuta Rylko, your teacher's assistant in Communication?"

"Oh, yeah! How you doin'?" His voice brightened.

"I'm sorry I'm calling so late, but I'm afraid I have a problem."

"What kind of a problem?"

"Well, it's the dumbest thing, actually. I feel a little stupid now, for calling you. . . ."

"Listen, do you want me to come over? Is there something I can do to help?"

"Oh, would you, J.J.? Gosh, that would be great."

"I'll be right there."

I gave him my address. Thirty minutes later he was knocking at the door. I hollered from the bedroom, "Come in!"

"Hello?" he asked, poking his head in the front door.

"I'm in here!" I called out to him.

He walked into the bedroom and stood frozen in the doorway, staring at the cast on my arm, the splint on my finger, the cast on my left leg, and the crutches leaning against the bedpost. I was still partially wrapped in the sheet.

"Hi," I said.

"Hi," he replied. "What happened to you?"

"I had a bad ski accident tonight. They say I'll be like this for at least six weeks. The crazy thing is, I can't seem to move. I mean, I can't use the crutches, I can't even budge off the bed!" I laughed, a little embarrassed at my predicament. "And I have to go to the bathroom."

J.J. stood there shaking his head, a big smile lighting up his face. "I'll bet you need someone to carry you in there!" He laughed gently.

"Well, yes, I guess I do."

With that, J.J. walked to the bed and carefully placed one arm under my cast and my other leg, the other arm around my back, and with a little effort, he heaved me off the bed and carried me to the bathroom. I stood there on my one good leg, wobbling, trying to keep the sheet wrapped around me, while J.J. slipped out and closed the door. A few minutes later, he carried me back to bed.

"This sheet isn't the best thing in the world to be wearing," he said. "Do you have something else you'd rather put on?"

"Well, I do, yes. I have a nightie in the drawer over there."

He brought the nightgown over to the bed, and with his eyes averted, helped me to put it on.

"How are you getting to class tomorrow? We're coming on midterm exams this week, you know."

"I hadn't even thought of that!" I said. "And I can't write!"

"Girl, you can't do anything!"

J.J. spent the night sleeping on the couch, all six feet, four inches of him. The next day, and for the next six weeks, he carried me into each classroom and then ran back to the car he parked illegally on the campus grounds to get my books. He picked me up after each class, sometimes sacrificing his own work, and brought me home. He cooked my meals, cleaned my house, and helped me into and out of the bathtub. Because of J.J., I passed my first year of graduate school.

J.J. was one of the most tender men I had ever known. Soon, I didn't see him as a black man. He became my best friend. He made me laugh. I learned that he had been an air force medic for fourteen years. He decided to quit the service after a bad marriage, and returned to school for his journalism degree at the age of thirty-four.

With J.J.'s guidance, my physical therapy sessions became challenges. J.J. was a track and field star, and he coached me into the use of whirlpool baths for my leg. Soon I was getting strong again—so much so that the next year, with two equal legs, I was skiing again.

Those six weeks turned into five years. We stayed together through school. We moved to Phoenix together for our first jobs at a television station. He was a news reporter, I was a camera operator. Two years later, we moved to San Francisco together.

Despite J.J.'s B.S. in journalism from the University of Colorado, and his background for relentless and thorough pursuit for a news story, he was given promises of numerous jobs with a "Don't call us, we'll call you next week and tell you when you can start." And the call would never come.

I had come home from another dead-end day and expected to hear, "Hey, babe!" Instead I found J.J., my eternal optimist with the ubiquitous smile, slumped over his typewriter. As he lifted his head I could see that this big, effervescent man had been crying.

"It's no use," he choked, "no one's going to call me. They never intended to. What do they want from me! What do I have to do?" He slammed his fist on the typewriter and fell over the keyboard, groaning and punching the carriage of the old Royal until he had no energy to hit it again. A few minutes later he was rolling a joint. He sucked in the soothing world of marijuana, and passed the joint along to me.

That week a producer from a radio news bureau called me. I had been referred to him by the manager of one of the news stations in town. I suspect the referral came, not because of my somewhat dubious talent, but rather to get me out of his hair!

This was a lasting lesson in persistence. I believe that just as one is about to despair, that is the time to kick one more time. Persistence is a struggle, but the struggle makes you strong.

So I became a ski reporter. My job was to call thirty radio stations around the state every morning and offer, free of charge, ski conditions at the major lodges in the Sierra. Stations could choose whether they wanted ten-, thirty-, or sixty-second sound bites and via phone, I would deliver. It certainly wasn't big time, but at least it was broadcasting! The position paid only three hundred dollars a month, and occupied my morning hours. That gave me the rest of the day to earn rent money by working at the San Francisco Racquet Club. My uniform consisted of a mini-skirt, white blouse, and a tray. So I worked as a broadcasting cocktail waitress for the next six months. J.J. began picking up free-lance assignments as a news photographer, and we got by.

Now, I wasn't your run-of-the-mill kind of ski reporter. When my colleagues were reciting the very serious side of skiing down the slopes, I was making a game of it. Instead of reciting a litany of poor skiing conditions at Squaw Valley, I'd make a poem out of it:

> Now for those of you who choose to,
> Skiing this week is a bummer,
> But if you can dig the after-ski life,
> You'll be sticking around till the summer!

I was no poet laureate, but the radio listeners loved it, and I became known as everybody's favorite ski bunny. People began to ask about me, wanting to know when the funny lady was coming on with the ski reports. The publicity grew and eventually, out of the thirty stations I gave thirty-second feeds to each day, five were asking me if I wanted to work for them in their newsrooms. Out of the five, the best offer came from KFMB in San Diego.

The news director wanted me as the afternoon news anchor during the peak listening hours known as "drive time," when everyone was homeward bound from work during rush hour.

I was working at the tennis club that afternoon when the bartender hollered across the room, "Hey, Danny, there's a call for you, long distance."

"Hello," I stammered, trying to balance nine full drinks and six ashtrays on the little plastic tray I had learned to hold above my head.

"Danuta Rylko? This is Fred Stemen, news director at KFMB radio in San Diego. So how soon can you start?"

"Start what?" I asked.

"Working for us," he said with a laugh in his voice.

"What!" I screamed. "What did you say?"

By this time all the other waitresses, half the clientele, and the bartender all rushed to my side, thinking there had been a death in my family.

"That's right," Fred grinned over the phone, "we're ready for you. When can you start?"

"When can I start? When do you want me?" I asked, hardly believing I was actually having this conversation.

"Well, let's see, this is Thursday—how about Monday? Can you make it by Monday?"

"Monday?" My mind went blank. I looked at the bartender, who by now had figured out that whatever Monday held, it would be good. He winked and nodded and punched me on the arm.

"Yes, yes, tell him yes, you can make it by Monday," he prodded me.

"Monday, yes, Monday, I can make it by Monday," I repeated into the phone. By now I was too numb to remember the rest of the conversation. I only knew my wildest dream had come true! My break had come. When I hung up the phone, I let out a yell and threw my tray with the nine drinks and six ashtrays in the air. The bartender leaped across the bar and hugged me. The waitresses all crowded around me and giggled their congratulations. The owner of the sport shop came running through the crowd, swung me around, and planted a kiss on my cheek. Even the club's patrons caught the congratulation fever. One member bought me a dozen roses and another a small piece of jewelry as a going-away gift.

Within the hour I had turned in the miniskirt and walked out of the club, vowing to never pick up a cocktail tray again.

Now I had to tell J.J. I was torn between happiness at my good fortune and empathy with his despair. But when I delivered the news, his dear face lit up like a bonfire and he wrapped big, strong arms around me and held me up in the air, grinning from ear to ear, not with his joy but with mine. This meant I was leaving and we both knew it, but we didn't talk about it. Didn't even hint at it.

J.J. helped me pack my few things: my cat, Nietzsche, my two African violet plants, a couple of books, and a suitcase of clothes. It was a dreary Saturday morning in San Francisco. The fog was heavy over the City by the Bay. I wanted to think it was the drizzle from the fog that was running down J.J.'s face when we said good-bye. Five years was a long time to spend loving someone. But the gap had widened over the last year.

When we spoke of marriage, I thought of the turmoil. Marriage was difficult at best, but a black man and a white woman would make it even tougher. People never let you forget. I had been called "nigger" by mere association. I felt the sting of an under-the-breath slur. I watched while store clerks helped others but somehow didn't see us. I saw J.J.'s pain on a daily basis and watched him struggle, with twice the effort of another man, for the same courtesies, simply because he was a man of a different color. I watched despair creep in on J.J. and saw him try to fight it off with a cheerful smile that lied about the torment going on inside him. This was not life. This was a battle of the worst kind—a battle of bigotry. It was a conflict I didn't have to encounter. It was an experience I didn't have to endure, a suffering I didn't love enough to sacrifice for.

I kissed J.J. and he clutched me and pulled me to him. Now we both had drizzle running down our cheeks. I stepped into my car and turned it south. In the rearview mirror, I watched J.J. turn his back and go inside the house.

This job was my turning point and I was racing toward tomorrow.

Chapter Two
Looking for Springtime

Kai's Story
February 1974

Winter is not gentle in Sweden. An icy wind blows off the Baltic Sea this time of year, chiseling away at the armor coating of the Swedish people, pinching them in, bending them over, lowering their vision, and limiting their expectations. Darkness hovers over the land, squeezing out the sun to a brief appearance on the horizon. Children see the light of day only on weekends. They wake up to the dark, and creep along the snowy streets to school. The light rises and wanes in a few short hours. When school is let out, it is already dark again, and the students have missed the sun. Dark clothing helps retain what heat there is, and except for the rosy tinge on runny noses and apple-red cheeks, there is little color left to the season.

Kai walked into this blast of arctic vengeance, clutching at his briefcase, bound for his Stockholm office. A short time before, divorced and bankrupt, the pillar of the Princeton community had become the town leper. Friendless, penniless, and exhausted, Kai left for Sweden to take inventory of his life. He very much needed to feel human again.

A young woman we'll call Helena found him in the thick of his chaos. She sensed his vulnerability and was warmed by the honesty of it. His anguish evoked her nurture; his vacuum became her obsession; his needs became her plunder. He was a man who needed mending, and she was the illusory stage for his healing.

Apartments in Stockholm are not easy to come by, often carrying waiting lists up to five years. Living with Helena was not only convenient but it was also a comfort to be with someone who offered him love. She was a vivacious joy for him.

"I'm a nurse. I work for Doctor Soursweet," she told him. "You know, he's the most prestigious doctor in all of Sweden!"

Every morning, after breakfast, Helena hurried to the closet to get dressed for work: white shoes, white stockings, white uniform and cap. After Kai left for work, Helena would hurry back to the bedroom, where she carefully removed the snow-white nurse's uniform and delicately hung it back in the closet, until the next day, when she would become a nurse again. For weeks, she kept up the facade of the professional working woman, thinking the story was a more attractive lure than the truth—the truth being that she was an unemployed florist.

"My father was extremely ill last year. He was hospitalized with a heart attack. I do worry about him," she confessed to Kai one day.

Months later, Kai met Helena's father. He remarked to Kai, "Thank God I've never been ill. I've never had to stay in a hospital!"

Helena's fantasies weren't used viciously. It was a creative impulse, an opportunity to manufacture a more secure world. Lying was a manipulative tool used to evoke sympathy from others and esteem for herself. Kai played into her game innocently, unaware of the web that was being woven.

"I can never have children," she had told him. "The doctors tell me it is impossible. It must be the birth-control pills they gave me. The doctors say they have made me permanently barren."

Two months later Helena was pregnant with Robin, a son. A year later she was pregnant again, with their daughter, Michelle. Kai's heart went out to them and he loved them dearly. Obligation to two new babies fueled Kai's already massive sense of guilt from having left behind his first family. To the outside world, the death of a man was more honorable an exit from a hopeless situation than leaving and living. Now guilt and duty made him stay with Helena and the new family.

They were married in San Diego, California, 1976, in a minister's office in a quiet ceremony with two friends as witnesses. It was the right thing to do, he told himself. The children needed a name and they needed a father, but so did his children in Princeton.

Kai's former company in the United States, a major insurance company, invoked a noncompete clause which stopped him from receiving a life income. In essence, the clause stated that he could not sell life insurance for another company, even if it was in Sweden, and his company did not sell a nickel's worth of life insurance outside of the United States and Canada. Kai felt both angry and disappointed that twenty-two years of serving the company as one of their top salesmen was now ending in a contract which controlled his life and his choices. He had no choice but to return to America and his job in an effort to preserve his substantial investment in the company.

He also felt a need to be near his first family, but he was duty-bound to his second family. Before the blur cleared, he had a new home in Stockholm, a new home under construction in Princeton, his first family's home in Princeton, an apartment in Princeton, and Helena's old apartment in Sweden. Shuttling between two countries, supporting two families and five homes, Kai found himself once again frantically trying to please others, heroically unselfish, leeched by choices he didn't want to make, committed to a life he didn't want to have.

God has given us a world full of choices. Each decision we make is strung to another decision and then another, until our life is a string of pearls, each pearl a choice. The quality of our life is then determined by the quality of its pearls. Choices are the substance of our reality, the stuff of life. However cruel, however bitter, however painful, whatever joy, our choices are merciless—they are free for the making, and in most cases, they are revocable.

Kai was still learning that, but meanwhile Kai's choices were slowly killing him.

This was a particularly blustery day in Stockholm, and the wind thrashed at the man lampooning the air with the thrust of his head, intent to push beyond the forces that held him. With each blast of wind his steps took a smaller bite forward. He was losing the energy to fight off this winter. It wasn't just the season. It was an entire lifetime of winters and wrong choices. It was never tasting springtime, his soul never stirred by summer.

He plugged two steps forward, the wind threw him one step back. Kai was tiring of this lumbering dance. He planted his feet like a boxer in his final round, and stood in the middle of the street, eyes squeezed shut, rocking in the wind.

"Oh, God," he moaned. "Oh, God, oh, God, where are You? Where am I? What am I doing here?"

Another blast slammed into him and he reeled back another step.

"Jesus!" He screamed through clenched teeth. "Jesus!"

The name took him by surprise. *Jesus* was a name he once knew many years ago. He had dedicated his life to that name then, but nothing much came of it. No magic formulas, no gold wand, no choir of angels. No significant changes, but then, he didn't expect anything, and he didn't grow beyond that day. He was never taught how to lay hold of God. He never knew the power of God, so he slowly slipped away from the name he now held in gritted teeth.

Jesus. His mind raced back to a book by Pat Boone. It was called *A New Song.* Boone told the story of a Jesus Kai had never known.

The wind slashed at him again, licking its icy tongue across his face. Kai was falling back with each new blast.

"Jesus. What about Him? What about Him that made Boone live again?" He tried to think. "Power. There was a power of God somewhere in that name, but where and how?"

The storm was in full fury. Snow streaked past him in horizontal lines and wind pierced him with little stab wounds. He stood battered on the outside, embattled within.

Pat Boone wrote about a God Kai had always hoped for. A God of passion, relentless in His desire to reach down to the tangled human soul. Here was a God of touch. A God of knowing. Tangible to the human intellect. There was a man in the book who showed Pat Boone how to achieve this terrifying intimacy. His name was Harald Bredesen.

Suddenly, from somewhere, a trickle of strength. A light was shining. Urgency swallowed him. Adrenaline was warming his blood, standing him up straight. He took a deep breath. He licked his cracked lips and opened his eyes. He was going to fight this storm.

A taxi sped by and he hailed it.

"Where to, mister?" the cabdriver asked, focusing on his new passenger in the rearview mirror.

"Take me to heaven!" Kai shouted.

"What's that?" the cabby asked.

"The airport," he shouted at the driver. "Take me to the airport!"

An hour later, equipped with only his briefcase, Kai Soderman was on a plane, destination Los Angeles, California. He was going to find Harald Bredesen, to find a God he needed more than life itself. He was going to find springtime.

Danuta's Story
March 1976

San Diego was intimidating. I was called to the big city to do a big-city job. I spent all my energy frantically trying to learn what to do, while pretending that I already knew what to do. I don't think I fooled anyone, especially Fred Stemen, the news director. Everyone called him Uncle Fred. He chaperoned the rookies through the web of news gathering, assimilating, and reporting with nothing short of love. He disguised his softness with a dirty-old-man role on the hip FM side of KFMB. His newscasts carried a benign lechery that was associated with a gravel-pit voice from too many cigarettes and too much late-night-newsman dedication that could frequently be observed after hours in the local tavern, and a sly wit that intricately implied more than he was saying.

While Uncle Fred was teaching me the ropes of radio news, I was at the same time the drive-time anchor for the AM side of the station. I boomed into the mike all the authority I could muster, hoping all the while that nobody would blow my cover. Nobody did, but my pretense of expertise cost me dearly. Each night I stood on the balcony of my rented condo by the beach in Coronado, watching my hands shake with the withheld anxiety of a full day. The condominium was in an exclusive area usually reserved for the rich if not the famous. I was neither, but I was working on both.

My immediate goal was to buy some furniture. It became annoying to have to sit on the john in order to write a letter on the bathroom counter, and sleeping on the floor got very old after the first six months. Lacking the basics inhibited entertaining. My first year in San Diego, I spoke to virtually no one from the time I left work Friday evening until the time I went to work Monday morning. No one called me and I called no one. I was exhausted much of the time and relished long, quiet weekends to myself, although there were times when I yearned for a little companionship. I put off loneliness by running up to eight miles a day on the beach. An occasional glass of wine helped smooth the rough edges, and a late-night cigarette with a glass of brandy before bedtime helped me sleep. During this hibernation I learned to sketch in charcoal, wrote volumes of poetry, and dabbled in metaphysical phenomena.

With a set of tarot cards I thought I could peer into my future. With my Transcendental Meditation I was able to peer inside myself. With a toss of three coins I could garner wisdom from the *Chinese Book of Changes*. And with a quick glance at the hand of a stranger, I could tell his past and his future, his strengths and his weaknesses. Yoga kept me in touch with my *shakras* (spiritually sensitive areas of my body). Vegetarianism kept my system free of toxins. My astrological flowchart filled in all the blanks.

I remember so well the day I was initiated into TM. I was instructed by my guru to spread a white sheet over an altar upon which I was to lay a bowl of rice, a few pieces of fresh fruit, some flowers, and a candle. These were to be gifts to the great teacher, Maharishi Mahesh Yogi, and all his spiritual ancestors. With a few words of mumbled Indian dialect, I was given my mantra and the name of a spiritual guide I could call upon if I felt the need for direction.

"Do you understand all that I have told you this evening?" my teacher asked me.

"Yes, thank you for your instruction," I replied, trying to sound very spiritual.

"There is just one more thing I think you must know before I go," he said rather mysteriously.

"Yes, master." I waited.

"There is what is known as unstressing."

"Unstressing?"

"It is a phenomenon of the technique I have taught you," he said. "It may happen that during your initial phase of TM you will find your body relieving itself of age-old tensions and anxieties that have intoxicated you spiritually. In other words, you may find yourself wetting the bed."

"Wetting the bed?" I could feel my face flush with embarrassment.

"Don't worry," he said. "It is natural."

I knew it was natural when I was eight months old, but I thought I had outgrown that by now. Nevertheless, I bowed respectfully, and that night, I unstressed.

I didn't know what I was looking for, but whatever "it" was, I looked for it with a passion. I had a lusty affair with life. I lived by episodes, each filled with its own vitality, every undertaking a matter of intrigue, every ordeal suffered in its own little microcosm. I lived molecularly, one atom at a time. I was a homogenized blend of contradictions, a million little complete lifetimes breathing one breath.

What I feared most was losing myself to mediocrity. I watched too many others living a humdrum existence. Cemeteries are filled with people who lived without passion, or without knowing why. I dreaded that finality. Somewhere in my past I determined for myself a life of full capacity. If there was no meaning, then let it mean celebration, exuberance.

I always believed there was a reason for being here, but I couldn't find any one purpose. But I sincerely believed that a truth existed, and there had to be more than what I was finding. At times, I turned my search from the spiritual to the sensual. I tried skydiving and race-car driving. I was a ski instructor, a swim instructor, a scuba diver. I learned to sail and bought a small sailboat. And I tried falling in love, dozens of times. It was not the men I loved as much as it was the falling in love itself. I loved the dynamics, the discomforts, the uncertainties, the uneasiness, the sleeplessness. It was the daze of love that I loved. If comfort set in, complacency usually accompanied it, and I could see the burner was cooling. I wasn't into cooling. I wanted the full flame, or nothing at all.

Secretly, I never believed love was a lasting ideal. I recognized only the transitory, fleeting splash of infatuation. I had never known the other. My attempts at finding a love faucet that stayed turned on unconditionally were as hopeless to me as someone who chases the horizon. Real love did not exist—not for me. Not ever for me. Underlying my idealism was a profound isolation. A part of me was sequestered from observation, left unexamined. I harbored monsters within me: desperation, loneliness, and a strange hunger to die.

My curiosity about life and death sustained setbacks as I looked for something tangible, something real, something . . . anything.

During my meditative hours in TM, I drew deeper and deeper within myself. I called my guru for advice.

"What are you finding, child?" he asked.

"Only my nothingness," I complained.

"But you have discovered the secret of the universe!" he delighted. "Something *is* nothing! Now if you really want something more, for fifteen hundred dollars I can teach you to levitate."

I hung up the phone. I had paid him three hundred dollars to learn that nothing really was something.

I eventually became a charter member of the Religion of the Month Club. Almost daily I was proclaiming to the newsroom crew that I had found another level of spirituality. One day it would be macrobiotics. The idea was that if one ate seeds indigenous to one's environment, one could reach spiritual maturity. San Diego didn't have a lot of seeds—a lot of fleas, but not a lot of seeds.

I was fitting into Southern California. Within the first year of my arrival I outfitted my condominium with beaded curtains, macrame wall hangings, incense pots, hanging baskets of plants, floor cushions, and a planter for my personal-use marijuana plants that were gaily growing on my balcony.

Within three years of working at the radio station, I was given several opportunities to launch into television. The opportunities came because I began to think of myself as a television personality, even though I was a radio personality. By that I mean that while other radio people would come to work in sweat shirts and blue jeans (after all, when someone's voice is the only thing going over the airways, who cares about what that voice is dressed in?), I would come to work dressed as though I were on television, in fully coordinated outfits. As I nurtured the belief that I was a TV person temporarily working in radio, others came to see me the same way.

Eventually, a position opened up for a weathergirl at KFMB-TV. I eagerly applied for the job. Management thought I would be worth a try.

My first weather forecast was given on the 6:00 P.M. news. I forgot the names of all the states. I forgot what state I lived in. Management reserved opinion on my talent, attributing the first night to the jitters.

The second night the only weather I found was a tornado in some small town in Texas. And I finished off the forecast in less than ninety seconds, three and a half minutes too soon.

By the third night I had pumped up my self-confidence, memorized the map, and pulled out every weather trivia item printed in the *Farmer's Almanac*. During the newscast, I was repeating my weather speech to myself over and over again: "Well, John, it certainly looks like the country is in for a hard weekend. The northeast has been under torrential rains for the past few days, and there's no end in sight. As for the Great Plains states, the drought is still continuing there. . . ." I was loaded for bear.

The news anchor turned to me and said, "Danuta, what's happening with the weather across the country?"

I didn't hear him. I was busy memorizing my speech, staring blankly at a spot somewhere off the set.

The anchorman repeated himself. "Danuta, I understand we have some weather news. . . ."

I think I was overloaded for bear. I was startled to hear my name called so soon. I was on! I was so full of facts and figures and vignettes that I forgot my opening line.

"Uh, oh, hi John, yes, we have weather all across this great country of ours. . . ." My brain hurt. What in the world was it I was supposed to say? Finally, the motor activity of my brain took over and I jumped up from the desk and walked over to the map. It looked so much bigger and imposing than I remembered it. States and names of towns all blurred together. I pointed ambiguously to the map with a trembling finger, and opened my mouth to say something. I lost my breath. I couldn't breathe! I began panting for air.

"What we hhhhaave hhhhere (gasp) is a situation thaaat (gasp) could be a situation for all these states (gasp) over here." I fluttered the back of my hand toward the map indicating some general area over Canada. I was hyperventilating. My voice trembled, my stomach felt funny.

"Now, for all these guys over (gasp) here . . ." I indicated with large circular motions the entire center of the country, ". . . (gasp) they have good weather . . . and, uh, Louisiana, thaaat's (gasp) somewhere down here, they haaave uh, something going on there. . . ." I was rummaging through all my notes, trying to remember what in the world it was about Louisiana I was supposed to say. The notes slipped from my hand and dropped to the floor. I quickly dropped to my knees to pick them up, and completely disappeared from the camera. I took the cameraman by surprise, and he tried to follow me. He tilted down to the floor, just as I popped back up. Now he was shooting my shoes.

"Uh, something quite bad is happening in Louisiana, probably a tornado, or a hurricane, or a flood, but coming closer to hooome (gasp), we have nice weather here, and nothing to worry about,

John." Gratefully I was back in my chair behind the desk, my hands neatly folded in front of me.

"Isn't there anything else happening in San Diego County overnight, Danuta?" John, the anchorman, prodded me.

"Oh! I'm glad you asked, ah, John. There is a flood watch out for the deserts and uh, oh, yes, there's a small-craft advisory for coastal waters . . ." it was all coming back to me now, ". . . and a severe storm watch over the county tonight. And, oh, there's a traveler's advisory for people driving in the mountains. But, uh, other than that, everything looks okay from here, John."

My career as a weathergirl lasted three days. I trudged back to radio for another year. But defeat and shame didn't stop me. Soon there was an opening on "Sun Up San Diego," the popular morning talk show on the CBS affiliate. This was the show that helped launch the TV careers of Sarah Purcell, who went on to "Real People," and Raquel Welch. I applied.

More than five hundred applications had come in from all around the country. One hundred were accepted. Fifty were reviewed. Twenty-five were filtered out. Ten people were invited to live auditions. I was one of the ten.

We were all asked to bring to the audition something from home that we could talk about for four minutes to indicate who and what we were. I was going to bring my cat. As they were counting me down, at ten seconds to my report I remembered. My cat! I forgot to bring my cat! Too late. The camera was rolling. I raised my hands to stop the audition and apologize for coming unprepared when an extraordinary thing happened. I looked at my hands, turning them around and back to the camera again.

"These hands are very capable hands. They are the hands that have pulled toggle lines on parachutes while skydiving. These hands have hoisted air tanks on my back to scuba dive. These hands have taught hundreds of tiny infants water-survival techniques. I have always had trouble keeping long, beautiful nails. My nails are constantly chipped and abused, because they are busy hands. These hands can rip out a five-minute newscast on an old Royal typewriter in three minutes. They have written poetry and short stories. They are not too small, but not very big. They are strong hands, but they are feminine hands as well. Most of all, these are Polish hands, because without them, I could not speak!''

I got the job. For the next five years, every morning I co-hosted ''Sun Up'' with Jerry G. Bishop, a popular disc jockey turned TV host from Chicago, taught infants to swim during midday, anchored radio news in the afternoon, and at times substituted on an evening radio talk show. My radio experience included news director at a local station, disc jockey at an oldies-but-goodies station, and news entertainment at another station. I was a busy woman. And I loved every minute of it.

''Sun Up San Diego'' was one of those magazine-format shows that dealt with local news events, cooking segments, authors on book tours, occasional movie celebrities, various astrologers, exercise segments, and animals from the San Diego Zoo.

I was always given the zoo animals because they liked me. The tarantula liked me a lot. Joan Embry of Johnny Carson and zoo fame handed the spider over to me with instructions not to move. I wasn't going to move with a tarantula on me if the worst earthquake were to strike and toss us into the sea. I froze solid. The huge spider was black and hairy and began to crawl up my arm. Joan kept talking nonchalantly about how harmless the spider was. The tarantula kept crawling, past my elbow, to my shoulder, too close, too close to my neck. I winced and he started down toward the breast pocket of my jacket and sat there like a huge black brooch. When Joan finally pulled the creature off me, I had ground my back teeth into my jawbone.

On another occasion, Joan delivered to the studio two almost fully grown spotted leopards. They were straining on thin leather leashes.

"Are you sure these guys are safe on those leashes?" I asked.

"No problem," Joan replied. That should have tipped me off, because the very next second, they jumped up on me to play. I screamed and ran off the set. The leopards snapped out of the trainers' hands, dragging their leashes behind them, and took off after me. I ran all around the studio screaming for help, while everyone else ducked behind the couch. If the cats hadn't slipped on the slick studio floor, I think I would have been history.

One of the ickiest things I did on the zoo segments was to help Joan hold a boa constrictor. The snake was at least fourteen feet long, and I volunteered to hold up the tail end. That way, I wouldn't have to look it in the face. While Joan was explaining how docile the creature was, the snake kept going limp on me and I would dangle part of the tail down and hold him closer to the center of his body. What I wasn't aware of was that the snake was slowly winding himself around me. By the time the segment was over, I was wrapped in boa.

That was panic enough, except I had a live sixty-second extemporaneous commercial to do, and we didn't have time to untwist the boa from me. From the waist up, I frigidly delivered a one-minute plug for a weight-loss clinic, while a boa constrictor was reducing me from the waist down.

Of all the crazy stunts I did, the most bizarre occurred during a high divers' championship we were covering live from Sea World. The tiny circus-sized ladder stretched seventy-five feet high into a dot in the sky, above the water tank that held Shamu, the killer whale. Actually, the tank was the home of three killer whales, but the Sea World people transferred the huge creatures to an adjoining holding tank. Shamu's tub was used for the diving event because it was the deepest pool in Southern California. During the event the divers were daring me to dive off the tiny platform that wagged in the wind.

"So, Miss Danuta, are you going to do it?" one of the divers asked me.

"I've got my bathing suit under this dress," I admitted. "And I can't look a dare in the face."

And with that, we went to a commercial break. The "floor manager," the person who gives the time cues and standby cues, raced up to me. "You've got exactly two minutes to climb up that ladder and dive into the pool before we have to close the show. Are you going to do it?"

"Of course I'm going to do it!"

I didn't know what I was saying. I started up that little-bitty narrow ladder in my thongs. I was halfway up when the floor manager yelled up at me, "Stand by, you're on the air in five, four, three, two, one. . . ." He pointed his index finger toward me.

"Hello, everybody! I'm on my way up to try the dive myself!" Just then a gust of wind blew by me and the ladder began to rock. I clung to it for dear life. I was almost to the platform, just three more rungs on the ladder. *I hate ladders,* I thought. I reached the platform. Some platform. It was simply a piece of wood, one foot square, the size of a kitchen tile. I stood on this little piece of wood, trembling in the wind, my back against the ladder for support. And then I looked down. That was a mistake.

Down was so far away. It was where I wanted to be, where I could look people in the eyes—from the sky, their faces looked like flecks of puffed rice staring up at me. I started to feel sick.

This was a stupid thing to do. I didn't know what to do next. I couldn't climb back down because I didn't know how. Besides, I hated ladders, and climbing down backwards is a lot harder than climbing up forward! I was trapped like a cat up a tree. And I was scared.

Suddenly I heard the voice of the floor manager: "Fifteen seconds to the close . . . it's now or never!" A surge of courage swept over me. This was television! This was live TV! The show must go on. I was the show. I had to jump! Now!

And with that, I lifted my heels from that little platform and was free, in the air, just the wind and my hair lifting up from my face, flying, floating. And then I lost the bottom of my stomach. It felt as though it dropped down faster than the rest of me—a sickening feeling, not to have your stomach with you at a time like this. *Ka-ploosh!* I hit the water with my feet. The soles of my feet burned. The shocking cold water gobbled me up. I was swallowed into a world of slow motion, a blue-and-white world of swirling bubbles. Down, down, I plunged to the bottom of the blue slow-motion world. The water wrapped around me like a blanket, soothing, reassuring. Everything was all right now. I was going to be okay. Touching bottom now, I had to spring up with my feet and then slowly drift to the top, where I could see the sky and the sun sparkling through the turquoise waves. . . .

I was halfway to the top when I saw Shamu. The Sea World trainers thought the show was over, and they let all three killer whales back in the pool. They were coming straight for me! I had visions of being eaten or crushed between their enormous bodies. I exploded through the top of the water.

"Hey!" I screamed. There wasn't time to holler again. Shamu was practically on top of me. I plowed through the water, stretching for the shore side of the tank with every stroke. Shamu was licking my feet! I reached the side and scrambled out of the water, coughing and choking, heaving with adrenaline.

"Doggone it! Who let the whales back in the pool!" I yelled. Somebody threw a towel in my face. They had miscalculated the time. We were still on the air.

Chapter Three
Falling in Love

Kai's Story
February 1974

Kai Soderman stepped off the Scandinavian jumbo jet, blinking into the California sunshine, carrying only his briefcase and wearing a heavy reindeer-skin coat that instantly became obsolete in the December heat of Los Angeles. It was a rash move, he was thinking, but the sun warm-washed his face and the dry, salty air smelled good. Whatever the compulsion, he had to follow it through. Amused sun-bronzed faces smiled at him as he struggled to take off his reindeer hide and headed to the rent-a-car desk. He had no idea how to find Harald Bredesen, but a church called Church on the Way was mentioned in Pat Boone's book. That was a beginning.

He found himself in a Wednesday-evening service. He hardly heard a word, his heart was pounding so in his ears. An altar call was given, and Kai was the first to run up the aisle. He had first

49

given his heart to Christ in 1957, but too many years without watering the soil had passed, and the intervening time was only a faded memory of a promise he had made so long ago. That night Kai recommitted his life to Jesus Christ. The elders took him to a prayer room in the back of the church and together they prayed for the Baptism of the Holy Spirit. Kai was kneeling and was quietly praying when one of the elders pronounced, "Praise God! Brother, you have received the gift of tongues!"

Everyone else in the room was shouting, "Alleluia! Praise the Lord!"

Kai found himself vehemently shaking his head and trying to explain, "No, no, that isn't my prayer language, it's my native tongue! I was just praying in Swedish!"

The following year, 1975, Kai and his family moved to California. During the next two years Helena would cross the Atlantic twice as she and Kai made numerous attempts to keep the family together. But there were too many lies and too many false starts. The marriage could not be brought back to life. Neither of them found the strength to keep it together.

Kai kept the next appointment with the marriage counselor and went alone. "Kai, what would you do if you could do anything that you, Kai Soderman, wanted to do? If you didn't have to please anyone else but yourself. Just this once, what would you do?" the counselor asked him.

Without hesitation Kai said, "I'd rent a condominium on the beach in Coronado."

"Then why don't you?" queried the counselor. "You've tried living for everyone else, and it hasn't worked. Try living for yourself for a change, and find out what it feels like."

That very afternoon, Kai found himself on a balcony overlooking the blue Pacific. He watched the sun set in a pastel-colored sea and woke up the next morning to see hundreds of dolphins playing in the tide. This was his first day of life, he decided. All his mistakes and all his problems from here on out were going to be of his own choosing. He was going to learn how to make choices for himself, and he would learn how to live with those decisions.

The end came one afternoon when Kai was delivering a check for food to Helena and the children. He found the driveway filled with cars. Inside the house, dozens of strangers were examining the fine handmade European furniture, and asking questions about the rugs. Every item in the house was marked with a price tag.

"Helena, what's going on here? Who are all these people?" he asked.

"They are buyers, Kai, and this is a garage sale. I've decided to sell everything. I'll give you half of everything, but I'm leaving for Sweden tomorrow. You can come with me if you want to. But it doesn't matter—I'm leaving."

That evening, Helena's father called Kai with a proposition. "Kai, you come back with Helena. You don't belong in the United States. You should come back here and live with your family."

"But what about my business?" Kai asked him. "I've just gotten started here. I'm a United States citizen. I've worked hard to get on my feet in California. I can't just leave. Besides, if I did, what would I do in Sweden?"

"It doesn't matter what you do," his father-in-law said. "You can come home and drive a taxi."

With unexpected emotion, Kai suddenly let loose a lifetime of fury. "Look," he shouted into the phone, as if arguing with himself. "I've had it with everyone running my life, telling me what to do and how to do it, where to do it and with whom to do it. I've had it with living a life that is not my own. I will not go back to Sweden. I will not close up my business here. And I will not end up busted and broken and driving a taxicab to make you people happy. This is my life. It is my happiness. And it is going to be my choice this time—not yours, not Helena's, but *mine!*''

Three years had passed since he first stepped off that airplane, and it was almost Christmas. He had never found Bredesen. He'd stopped looking. But things were about to change. That Sunday in church he happened to sit next to an elderly woman who commented on his fine singing voice. After a short conversation, Kai told her he had been looking for Bredesen but understood that he was now living in Vancouver, Canada.

"Not anymore," the woman said. "I'm the organist in his new church in North County!" She gave him Bredesen's address.

A phone call confirmed he was home and yes, he would see a visitor. Kai was breathless with anticipation when he rang the doorbell of Bredesen's North County home. A voice hollered out that the door was open and to come in. There was no one in the room, and Kai stood awkwardly in the hallway, shouting, "Hello?"

"I'm in here," a voice replied.

Kai followed the voice. Just then a short, brown man raced out of a side bathroom, girded only in a towel, and plowed right into Kai.

"Oh, you must be the person I'm expecting," Harald said.

Kai introduced himself. "Kai Soderman, Harald, and this truly is a great pleasure for me to meet you."

"Oh, yes, it is so very good to meet you, Kai. Won't you join me?" Harald asked.

"Join you? Join you where, how. . . ."

"Oh!" Harald exclaimed. "You see, my wife and my son are out shopping and my secretary is away for the day and I have the house to myself, so I thought I'd relax a little while in the Jacuzzi. Would you care to join me?"

"Well," stammered Kai, not sure how to proceed, "I didn't bring my bathing trunks with me and—"

"Oh, that's no problem," Harald said. "I have a pair you can wear." And he disappeared, only to reappear holding a rumpled pair of blue swimming trunks.

They marched out to the backyard, Harald serendipitously leading the way to the Jacuzzi with Kai in tow. Harald slipped in the bubbling froth as Kai stood there with the trunks in his hand.

"I guess this is rather unnecessary," he chuckled. He tossed the trunks aside and gingerly stepped into the hot water.

There they sat for the good part of an hour, Kai pouring out his heart and his hopes, relating the story of how he had come to California to find the man in the Jacuzzi.

"Oh, God, how good You are!" Harald shouted. "You don't mind if I take a station break every now and then, do you, while I praise the Lord?" Harald laughed.

Kai liked him. There was something genuine and unaffected in his manner. He had a childishness about him that held no pretensions, yet he carried the reputation of a spiritual giant on the forefront of the Charismatic movement. In one encyclopedia Harald Bredesen's face accompanies the explanation of *Charismatic*. Here was a man who had ministered to Arab heads of state. During the famous Camp David Peace Accord with Menachem Begin, Anwar Sadat, and President Jimmy Carter, Harald Bredesen was to be called upon to compose a prayer that the Arab, the Jew, and the Gentile could agree upon for the success of the peace agreement in the Middle East. When Sadat was assassinated, Bredesen would be the only non-Arab to walk behind the casket during the funeral. Sadat had learned to call Harald friend, and the two had many special hours together in Cairo.

Harald Bredesen had befriended Pat Robertson when the young minister was living and ministering in the poverty-strewn section

of Bedford-Stuyvesant in New York. Bredesen and Robertson
had remained close from that time on.

Here was Harald Bredesen, the counselor to prime ministers
and presidents, smiling and chortling, throwing back his head in
laughter, sitting in a bathtub with a virtual stranger. Suddenly his
eyes burned into Kai. He knew what Kai had come for.

"Kai, may I ask you a question?"

"Yes, surely, Harald," Kai said.

"Do you know about the Holy Spirit?" Harald asked.

"Well, Harald, I have heard about the Holy Spirit, but I'm not
sure I understand how that works."

"Kai, do you believe that the Holy Spirit works today as He
did in the day of Pentecost?"

"Yes, I do, I think," Kai answered. "There is power there,
power to live the way Christ wants us to live. But can anybody
have it?"

"You can indeed have that power of the Holy Spirit in your
life," Harald beamed. "Will you pray with me?"

Harald didn't have to ask twice. That afternoon, Kai was bap-
tized in the Holy Spirit, and for the first time in his life he began
praying in tongues. He found the power of Christ in man in
Harald Bredesen's Jacuzzi.

Five days later Kai met Danuta.

Danuta's Story
December 17, 1977

The elevator door opened on the fourteenth floor and he stepped
into my life. I had seen him before in the building, and even
asked the doorman for his name. The doorman said the same

gentleman had already asked about me! And now, here we were, face-to-face, alone. My heart was flying as the elevator doors closed for the eternal journey to the ground floor.

He was carrying his guitar to a Christmas party, where he had been asked to sing. I was carrying my mandolin, rented only minutes before from a local music store. I was determined to teach myself to play "Lara's Theme" from *Dr. Zhivago.* Grasping the opportunity to speak, he turned, and with a dazzling smile said, "Oh, I see you play the mandolin?"

Overcome by dazzle, I lied and said yes.

"Well," he said, as the elevator doors opened at the lobby, "have a very good Christmas. Good-bye." And he left through the parking-lot door.

I was numbed by our conversation. I had said only one word, *yes,* but that one word was packed with dynamite. I meant yes with every fiber of my being. Here was a man in every serious sense of the word. I imagined hanging on his arm at the ball, nodding to the courtiers and curtsying to the queen. I could be regal with him, a princess of some exotic country ennobled by his charm. Here was a man who could be a statesman, or a duke, or at the very least, a knighted member of the royal Swedish court. He was tall and his shoulders were broad, his hair silver gray. His eyes hinted at some deep sadness. He was perfect. He was beautiful. I imagined him running after me with a glass slipper I had just lost. . . .

"Is this the tree you were looking at?" a voice barked, rudely waking me from my reverie.

"What? Oh, yes. The tree. Fine. Fine. That's a fine tree. I'll take it. Can you flock it heavily with snow and wrap it on my car, please?"

With the money exchanged and the tree flocked to look like a white Christmas in Southern California, the man with the barking voice slammed the tree on the roof of my tiny sports car, completely obliterating my vision both fore and aft. I drove home by feel. I was still wondering when I would see Prince Charming again when I turned into the garage and there he was, driving toward me! He was on his way out, I was on my way in. He slowed down as we passed each other and rolled his window down. I stopped and rolled down mine.

"Would you mind very much if I were to call on you sometime?" he asked.

I was cool. "Oh, no, I wouldn't mind at all. I'd love it! I mean, yes, that would be wonderful!"

That was our second conversation. My heart was all over my shirt.

But now I had a more practical problem to deal with. I had to get the tree upstairs. I lived on the sixteenth floor and there were only two passenger elevators, fully carpeted. I dragged my tree in on a sheet, hoisted it upright, leaned it, with some encouraging bending, against the side of the lift, and pushed the button for the sixteenth floor. Minutes later I was dragging the tree by its trunk down the hall, leaving little telltale flocked needles behind me on the cushioned pattern of carpeting that led directly to my condominium.

Inside, I discovered that an eleven-foot tree didn't fit under an eight-foot ceiling. I had to eliminate at least three feet of tree without a saw. I was a city girl. I didn't own a saw but I had the next best thing, or maybe the next best thing to the next best thing: a bread knife. I straddled the flocked branches of my tree and hacked away at the beefy trunk with my narrow aluminum JC Penney bread knife, as it wobbled and stuck and finally snapped inside the wood. Figuring I had to retrieve the blade before I could find another bread knife, or borrow my neighbor's, I was now lying down beside the tree, trying to pry the blade out with a small steak knife. It wasn't working. I had rolled under the tree looking for a better angle, spitting out needles and phony snow, when the doorbell rang.

I wriggled out from under my semiamputated tree, flocked from nose to toes, pine needles sprouting out of my hair, drenched in perspiration from my considerable effort, and opened the door. And it was him!

He stood before me decked out in all his elegance, and I stood before him decked out in pine needles.

"Oh," he said, "have I called too soon?"

"Nooo," I cried. "Not at all."

"Well, I was wondering if you might like some dinner."

"I'd love dinner!" I replied. "I'll be ready in ten minutes."

Twenty-one days later, I was in love with him.

Our Story
December 18, 1977

"What are your goals in life, Danuta?" Kai asked.

I wiggled sand between my toes and caught a sea breeze that splashed up into my face. This was the first of many conversations we had on that beach in Coronado, but it was the most significant. The beach was an opportunity to see a lot of each other without having to come up with a special occasion every time. Walking along the beach had other benefits as well; there were few distractions, and the long silences made room for reflective words and meaningful nods. Earth, wind, and sky incubated our moments. We were every bit a part of the elemental forces swirling around us. We were honest with each other.

"When I was a little girl and people would ask me that question, my answer was always an astonishment for them," I said, smiling shyly.

"Then I want to know even more than ever. What do you want to be when you grow up?" he chuckled.

"Well, when I was a little girl, my answer was that one day I would be a sort of foreign correspondent who traveled the whole world trying to make people love one another. I know that sounds like the answer a child would give, but for some reason, my answer now hasn't changed much. I may have lost some of the naivete since then, but the idea still seems to be the same. One day I see myself negotiating peace between nations, as an ambassador of some kind—perhaps in the midst of a great world crisis, or the aftermath of crisis, I'm not sure. But anyway, that's my answer. It's not very simple, is it?" I hoped he understood what I was saying.

"What do people say now when you tell them that?" Kai asked.

"Well, actually, I've never told anyone that before. In fact, this is the first time I've ever really put these thoughts into words. I'm a little amazed at myself," I confessed. "Usually I say something like, 'Oh, I guess I'd like to work for one of the networks one day.' But I don't go around exclaiming Napoleonic ideas." We both laughed, but Kai quickly became serious again.

"I don't think what you've said is too grandiose," he said. "I think that of all the people I've ever met, you are the most capable I have known." He stopped there for a moment, a long moment, gathering some distant thoughts. "I will tell you this," he said, "I feel a deep conviction that will happen. I'm not an idealist, but for some strange reason, I believe it. I believe that what you have said will come true." Kai stopped there, feeling an awkward need to support my dream. But he didn't understand that feeling any more than I understood the prophecy I had just spoken.

Kai felt awkward for another reason. He was gun-shy of another relationship, following so soon on the heels of his second marriage. He was not yet divorced from Wanda, and there was much to resolve from his past before he could look forward to the future.

Kai's reticence only endeared him more to me. Here was an honest, gentle man, who had been through a great deal of pain, who had a wonderful calm about him, who spoke in velvety tones, whose hands were long and slender and sensitive to the frets on his guitar and to the touch of my hand. I learned so much about him in a few short days.

One soft night, he told me the story of how his father, in a drunken blur, tried to push him in front of a midnight train that roared through an isolated station in a snowy little village above the arctic circle. He was only thirteen years old. There was no one in the station. He said he remembered seeing the frosty air shooting out of the smokestack, turning into billows of white clouds bouncing off the shine of a blue moon.

The roar of the train screaming toward him increased with the relentless push of his father's hand on the back of his neck. As the train tore past, he managed to kick free from his father's grasp. For years he remembered that incident with torment and confusion, and had told no one what had happened—not even his father.

At once I saw a frightened little boy, wanting love and approval from his disciplinarian father. That love came later, as father softened toward son, and their relationship flourished. I imagined a young boy who grew up looking at the sky, wondering what it held and who made it. A little boy who ran away from home a dozen times, one time crossing the border into Finland and then attempting to cross into Murmansk, Russia, trying to smuggle himself on board a boat destined for America. He spoke nostalgically of growing up in Lapland, listening to the snow crunching under his skis with a full moon flooding the forest during a midnight cross-country trek as a Boy Scout. A boy with a lot of hope, transformed into a man who still hoped, who searched for "something more in life." I was looking for that, too.

It was so easy to fall in love with him. And I had to tell him. But I had to find the right moment to pull out my heart and offer it to him. I was so terribly afraid that he didn't feel about me the same way I felt about him. But love is love and it must be told without hope of reward or reciprocity. If I didn't tell him, this tension would dangle in the air between us, invisible and ashamed.

The moment came during dinner in a little French restaurant in Coronado. Christmas lights mixing with candlelight washed us in warm, rosy shadows. We held hands across the table. Awkward silences punctuated episodes of chatter, like explosions of words inside us, words we hoped to say but dared not.

"Kai," I said, trying to build up some courage by saying his name. "Kai, I have something to tell you, and I hope you won't be offended. Gee, this is going to be harder than I thought it would be. . . . These last few days have meant so much to me, and I think it's only fair to tell you that I like you very much, very much. In fact, I think I'm falling in—"

"Danuta, before you say anything, I think you ought to know that I'm leaving. I'm going back to Sweden."

His words fell all over me. I felt them like harpoons: *leaving— Sweden—going.*

"What did you say?" I tried to smile as if I wasn't dying.

"I'm sorry," he said, as though he read my mind. "I have to go back to Sweden. I have a wife and a family I must try to pull back together. My brother has a business there and he needs me to help with it. Danuta, I never lied to you. You did know I had obligations.''

I thought I'd stopped breathing. I was still spinning from the blow of his first few words . . . *I'm leaving.* . . . I was dazed, staring straight ahead of me, looking at nothing. I think my mouth was open, with my unfinished sentence hanging in midair. Frozen.

He squeezed my hands. I woke from my stupor and smiled weakly. "Oh, yes. Well, of course. I mean, it was so unexpected." I smiled thinly, hiding my disappointment.

"It has been on my mind for some time now," he said. "I must try to reconcile with Helena one more time. You understand, don't you?" He was almost urgent for me to understand.

"Yes, of course I understand," I lied. I forgot the rest of the evening. Our conversation dulled and I guess we just went home. We stepped into the same elevator and drifted to our respective homes, he to the fourteenth floor and me to the sixteenth.

Inside my apartment, safe from the struggle of showing a brave smile, I cried. Once again, love had eluded me. What must I have been thinking—that I could fall in love and live happily ever after? Me? I began feeling sorry for myself, and worse, I felt betrayed by my own standards. After all, I was the girl who didn't believe love existed past infatuation, and once again this was proof that I was right. But I was hurting. So I lit some candles in the living room, pulled out my poetry book, and began to write:

> An imp
> Wrapped in blue eyes
> A Christmas present
> Trimmed in smiles
> Soft thunder
> In the winter rain

And twenty days
With a twinge of pain.
Chopin and brandy,
Tea and cheese,
And the tease of love,
That fits like a glove,
But flies like a dove
Out of hand.

In twenty days,
You hold my gaze,
And your image stays
As though I glimpsed at the sun
And was blind for a time.
I've held moments of you
In slow motion—a crime,
That each picture of you
Is the last this time.

Like that transparent stretch of flesh
On a newborn's head—
Love is easy to bruise.
As hard as I can,
I'll try not to cry,
But rejoice in your life,
As the butterfly flies.
My darling,
My imp,
My gossamer man.
Take care and breathe easy,
And write when you can.
Sweet Kai, Good-bye.

I read the poem to him, and we cried. Two days later he was
gone.

Chapter Four
Starting Over—Again

Kai's Story
1978–1979
Stockholm, Sweden

*F*our o'clock in the morning, in the dark, standing up to his ankles in snow, wearing only his pajamas under his coat, watching a miserable little puppy consider whether or not to pee in a blizzard, was not exactly Kai's idea of the promised land.

A perfect metaphor for my life, he thought, as he watched the mutt finally burn a yellow hole in the snow, spraying some of his business into Kai's open boot and down his foot. Kai had worked hard the past months, but the infamous Swedish tax burden took an enormous bite out of the profits, leaving him little for his efforts. This added extra strain to an already tense situation with Helena. The foundation of the marriage was slowly rotting away any hope for recovery. Disappointment and depression were taking a heavy toll.

He moved out of the house and found himself a small flat near the center of town. Then he saw a doctor about his despondency. He was given a prescription for a strong relaxant, with instructions to take four pills every twenty-four hours. With a glass of wine he washed down one pill, and waited impatiently for the pain of failure to subside. Thinking that two pills would work faster than one, he took another, and swallowed it down with another glass of wine. The toxic mixture of wine and drugs began to make him light-headed, as he sipped a third glass of wine with a third pill. That's when he stopped counting. Forgetting he had taken each subsequent pill, by the end of the evening he had ingested sixty-six of the one hundred pills in the bottle. The last thing he remembered was watching the wall of his room come crashing down on top of him.

The phone, knocked from the hook, floated in front of him, seductively out of reach. He struggled to raise his head and through the blur that was rapidly closing him in darkness, he clawed at the air, trying to stretch his deadened body to the telephone. When he was found twenty-four hours later, unconscious and turning blue, the palm of his hand was puffed up with an enormous blister from scratching at the air.

The man should have died, but for a peculiar incident. During the night, Inger, Kai's sister-in-law, had a vision. She saw Kai's face in an oval frame, gasping for air. Surrounding his face were the multiple faces of strangers, all blowing air toward him as though trying to help him breathe. The vision was so intense that Inger insisted on rousing her husband, Bo, and calling Kai. A perpetual busy signal over several hours flagged danger, and they rushed to his apartment.

Kai was hospitalized for two days, suffering from pneumonia, oxygen depletion, and a drug overdose. Emotionally and physically exhausted, he gathered together what little money he had and left Sweden, and Helena, permanently. They divorced a few months later. Worried that this singular incident suggested a drug-and-alcohol dependency, he checked into a rehabilitation farm in Pennsylvania for thirty days, and afterward, to assess his future and get his feet back on the ground, he found himself in a halfway house, penniless, homeless, and without a friend in the world except for one. And he wrote her a letter:

June 1979

Dear Danuta,

I am finally back in the United States, but not the way I had hoped. I have been spending the last month in a halfway house, after a thirty-day program at a rehabilitation farm in Pennsylvania for drug-and-alcohol dependency. Although they have not diagnosed me as an alcoholic, I came to be sure.

This halfway house is not a pretty sight. I share a room with a former bank robber and I clean latrines with a man who was accused of killing someone with a wrench at the age of twelve. He says he did it to protect his little sister from being raped, but the jury didn't believe him. Years later, the judge reversed the decision and let him out.

Some people here are angry, illiterate, and tired. I'm just tired. Life has been such a battle. I'm not sure where I'm going from here, or what I'll be doing. But I'm so glad to be back in America for a new start. I just needed to be in touch with you. Thank you for being there.

Love,
Kai

June 1979

Dear Kai,

I received your letter today, and was so very happy and excited to hear from you!

You sound like you're really down in the dumps, but I know you a little bit, I think. And I think you're a winner.

A man with your talents and abilities can never be put down for very long. You have strength—a spiritual strength that I envy.

Everybody has temporary setbacks in life. This could be a brand-new opportunity for you to make a brand-new start. You have dignity and resolve. You are one of the kindest men I have ever known. You have unique and wonderful talents with music and with business. You can do anything you want to do. I have faith in you.

Next time you get to California, I would be thrilled to see you again. Let me know your plans.

With love,
Danuta

That letter breathed new hope into Kai. He read it a dozen times. He was amazed that nowhere did she elaborate on his perceived illness. *She was right*, he thought, *I am going to make it.*

A call to a former client in Philadelphia was warmly received. The man loaned Kai three hundred dollars and the use of his car to drive to the customs office in New Jersey to pick up his belongings. Kai had written his first wife a letter from the halfway house telling her his story and saying he had used her address as his former residence. He asked that she acknowledge the receipt of his belongings from Sweden and that she send the receipt to him so he would have it to pick up his things at the port of call. When she received the receipt, she scrawled "Not Here" across it, and sent it back to Sweden. Without the receipt, Kai had no proof that his belongings were actually his. Standing in the customs office, Kai tried to explain to the clerk what had happened.

"Look, I'm in a bit of a bind here. You see, my ex-wife refused to accept the receipt and she sent it back to Sweden. You have everything I own in that big crate back there, and I need it."

"Do you have any other kind of ID?" The clerk asked, eyeing him suspiciously.

"All I have is my driver's license," Kai said, pulling at his pocket for his wallet.

"Nope," the clerk said. "A driver's license won't hack it. I need a credit card, or the receipt."

"I don't have a credit card yet," Kai apologized. "You see, I'm starting off new in America, and I haven't gotten back on my feet yet. . . ." His voice trailed off, seeing the unflinching bureaucrat was untouched by his story.

Meanwhile, in the back of the room, munching on a cigar, was a big, unkempt man sitting behind a desk, listening in on the conversation. "Dees women are always screwin' things up for us guys," he mumbled in a gravel-pit voice. "Give da fella da box."

The president of a financial-planning firm in California, knowing Kai's national reputation in the business, offered him a job. Kai was heading back to California. But first he was going to see Danuta. He could never get her completely out of his mind. She was like a beacon to him, representing life and hope, warm sunshine and healing.

And Danuta was waiting for him.

Our Story
July 1979

I was so happy to see him, I hardly recognized his weariness. His eyes lit up when he saw me. He opened his arms as wide as he could, and I was swallowed up in him. It was almost as if he had never been gone.

He had four days to spend in Southern California before he was due in Lake Tahoe, and we decided to go to Baja. We drove in my little white-and-orange-striped Porsche 914 and took the sunroof off. Even though the day was cloudy and overcast, the air was warm and dry, and the rush of wind against our faces felt free and good. I love to drive. I learned how to race cars in Anchorage, Alaska, from a boyfriend who raced on ice, and I usually take to the road like I mean business. Having Kai next to me, the open road to Mexico, and an open sports car was just about heaven. We laughed and talked about everything.

We prayed that if God was listening, would He please open a small hole in the thick shroud of clouds, and let the sun shine through it just on us. Kai insisted that God would hear. I insisted that positive thinking would compel the clouds to move. When a bright blue hole appeared above us we both grinned, assured that however that little hole got there, it was meant to be. It had to be.

It was during that drive that Kai reached out his hand and caressed the wrist of my right hand as it rested on the gearshift, ready to downgear on a curve or charge a slower car in front. During that tender moment, Kai fell in love with me. Or perhaps it would be more accurate to say he fell in love with my wrist first, and the rest of me quickly followed.

We stayed in a romantic old Mexican resort hotel called Rosarito Beach. Summer was over and the crowds had all left, leaving us the only couple in the huge resort, with an army of waiters, waitresses, busboys, pool attendants, and an entire orchestra for dinner and dancing. We danced all night, just the two of us in the middle of the floor, in Baja California, oblivious to the smiles and whispers from the hundred or more employees all around us. They called us honeymooners, and we didn't argue with them.

Kai rented a couple of horses in the morning for a ride through the surf on the beach. We walked miles in the sand and slept in the sun. In those four days we cemented a friendship that was to endure the hills and valleys of another three years.

Returning home, we ate in a small restaurant in Tijuana where, we were informed, the first Caesar salad was perfected.

I spoke about it first. "I know you're leaving again."

"It is a beginning for me, Danuta," he smiled. "And I have you to thank for that." He reached across the table and held my hands.

"Anytime, anywhere, you can call on me and I'll be there for you," I promised.

"Anytime, anywhere," he repeated, "I will be there for you."

I was to call on that promise six months later.

My interest in the occult was continuing, and if I couldn't sleep at night, I would sit on my living-room floor and write poetry by candlelight, sipping a small glass of brandy, or meditate on my mantra, trying to reach for some spiritual comfort that I knew was there but didn't know how to tap. It was during one evening after meditating that I sensed an increasing oppression come around me. It was darkness within the twilight of the room. It grew until it was darkness within darkness. The air felt thick and sickly heavy, and I began to gasp for every breath. I felt as if I was being watched. I suddenly became paranoid and jumped at any little sound. The hairs on the back of my arm stood on end, and I was frightened. I did not have to consider for a moment whom I should call.

"Hello?"

"Hello, Kai?"

"Yes, Danuta, are you all right?"

"I don't know. I'm sorry to call you so late at night, but something is happening and I don't know what it is."

"Calm down, and tell me what's going on." Kai's concern was mounting with every moment.

"Well, I don't know, it's just that I feel there's somebody here, or something here. I can't seem to get up on my feet, and it's hard to breathe. I'm scared, Kai."

"Oh, my darling, I wish I could help you. Should I get on a plane tonight?" he asked.

I heard a woman's voice in the background. "Who is that on the phone?"

"Oh, I'm sorry," I said. "I don't mean to interrupt you if you have company." I suddenly felt like a pain in the neck.

"It's all right," Kai said to the voice. "It's a friend of mine, and she's in trouble."

Returning his attention to me, he said, "Now tell me what you've been doing."

"Kai, I've just been meditating and writing some poetry, and suddenly this awful depression just swamped all over me." I began to cry.

"Danuta, I want you to let me do something for you. I want to pray for you. Will you let me?"

"Yes," I sniffed, "that would be okay."

"Dear Lord," he began, "put your loving arms around Danuta and hold her close to you. Protect her. And by the authority of Christ I rebuke Satan from her midst and any spirits that may surround her at this moment. And I speak peace to her in the name of Jesus of Nazareth. Amen."

"Amen," I whispered into the phone, hardly believing the sensation of warm honey that settled upon me. Within a second of that prayer, the air cooled and the oppression lifted. The name *Jesus* sounded so sweet and infinitely serene. Comfort overwhelmed me. I took a deep breath.

"Are you all right?" Kai asked.

"Yes, it's wonderful," I purred into the phone. "Thank you so much. Thank you so much."

"If you still need me, I can fly down tomorrow."

"No, Kai, you don't have to do that. Honestly, I suddenly feel just wonderful!"

"Kai, how long are you going to be?" It was that woman's voice again, and she sounded irritated.

"That's Vicky," Kai volunteered, sounding apologetic. "She's someone I've been dating out here. . . ."

"Kai, please, you don't have to apologize," I assured him. "I'm seeing someone as well."

"Oh," was all he said.

"I appreciate your friendship, Kai. Thank you for your prayer."

"Danuta, remember Mexico. Anytime. Anywhere."

I smiled. "Anytime. Anywhere."

That night I slept soundly, surrounded by an invisible network of angels. Kai did not sleep as well. Love was keeping him awake. He had to get back to Coronado.

Chapter Five
Best Friends

Kai's business as a financial consultant expanded, and with it came the luxury of moving back to Coronado, back to the fourteenth floor of my building. Several years had passed and he had completed a full circle. I was still living on the sixteenth floor, and our friendship was as strong and durable as ever, with one little exception: Kai was in love with me. But I was no longer so sure that I was in love with him.

There had been so many delays in this relationship. So many hopeful starts, and then sudden departures. I didn't want to hurt again. I didn't want to write another good-bye poem to him. I did not want to feel the sting of emptiness if he should leave again. And so I distanced myself from him emotionally, even though we were now closer in friendship and proximity. I loved meeting his children when they came to visit, and over the years I grew to love each of them. I continued to date other men, and he occasionally had dates with other women, although he scarcely spoke of them. I was not so reticent about my relationships and often spoke of them to him.

"Let me see my ocean!" I gushed at him frequently when I rang his doorbell. I would run to his balcony overlooking the turquoise sea, and breathe in the ocean air. My condominium was situated on the other side of the building, overlooking the bay and the skylights of downtown San Diego. This way I enjoyed both views. Kai always greeted me with loving enthusiasm. He acted as if he were seeing me for the first time in years. When problems were too big for me to handle on my own, when life was too complicated to cope with, if something wonderful had just happened to me, or if I was bored, I would call Kai, and he was always there.

It wasn't always convenient for Kai to see me. On more than one occasion, my call came at an awkward moment.

"Hello?"

"Hi! It's me!"

"Oh! My goodness! Hello!"

"I know it's late, but I just got in, and I'm feeling a bit upset. I had an argument with Dene. Can I come down for a little TLC?"

"Of course you can. Of course. Uh . . . five minutes?"

"Five minutes. You got it."

The next five minutes on the fourteenth floor was a flurry of activity.

"Look, uh, Sandra, that was a friend of mine, and uh, she needs to talk to me, and uh . . . well, I think we should get together some other time."

"Well, I don't know, I just got here a few minutes ago. . . ."

"Yes, I'm awfully sorry, Sandra, but this is an emergency. Where's your sweater?"

"I don't have a sweater."

"Oh, then your purse. Don't forget your purse." Perspiration was beginning to form on his upper lip as he counted down the minutes until the doorbell would ring.

"Thank you, Sandra. I'll call you," he promised as he hustled her out the door.

With Sandra gone, Kai tore around the living room, picking up any shred of evidence that another woman had occupied the space I was going to enter within seconds. Two glasses were quickly hidden as the doorbell rang.

"Hi!" I grinned at him. "Let me see my ocean."

"Oh, darling, you look wonderful! Boy, it's so good to see you! Come in. Come in." He ran his fingers back through his hair, trying to regain his composure, feeling uncomfortably like a guilty husband who had just hidden his mistress under the bed.

I never let on that I always knew when he had a date. On his television set he had an eight-by-ten color photograph of me with the inscription, "To the man I love, Danuta." Whenever he had a date, he put my picture in his bedroom, or in a drawer somewhere. That night, my picture was not on the television set. But for the most part, Kai seldom hid his love for me from anyone. All of his girlfriends knew he loved me. I was all he talked about when he took them out. He was a boring date.

My relationships weren't always such guarded secrets, since I did not harbor hope for a more personal relationship with Kai, as he did with me.

On the sixteenth floor, just next to the elevator, lived a sprightly seventy-eight-year-old retired vice admiral. The admiral had asked me to dinner one evening, and I accepted his invitation. He walked with a spring in his step when he was with me, and enjoyed introducing me to his friends and showing me a scrap-book of his duty in the Pacific during World War II. The admiral had been married and divorced five times and was once again alone in the world. He said I gave new meaning to his days. I liked the idea that he needed me.

One afternoon the admiral left a rose pinned to my door, telling me he loved me. It was the same afternoon that Kai and I had a dinner date. Kai came to the door and saw the rose and picked it off the door, thinking it was from me. As he stood there, grinning at the small and precious gift, a door down by the elevator opened. The admiral stuck his head around it and stared at Kai, making Kai feel a little uncomfortable.

"Hello!" Kai called out to him.

"Evening," The admiral gruffed back, and slammed the door.

When I told Kai I had seen the admiral a few times, he couldn't believe his ears. Meanwhile, the admiral assumed Kai was a friend of my mother. Life did get complicated. Later the admiral would ask me to marry him, and I considered his proposal for a time. Kai's frustration with me escalated.

I must admit I confused him. At one time I suggested that perhaps we might forsake all others and go steady. Kai was ecstatic! He called all of his girlfriends and told them he would not be seeing them anymore. He broke future dates with some of them, telling them that Danuta and he would be seeing each other exclusively from now on. Four days later I joined a computer dating firm.

I tried to explain that this was a research project for my tele-vision show, "Sun Up San Diego." The idea was that I would go through the computer dating process and then, finding the guy I liked the most, go for a date and bring him on television to talk about the experience.

Three months later I was still dating four of my selections. One day there was a telephone call from the fourteenth floor.

"What about dinner tonight?" Kai asked.

"Oh, I can't, Kai, I have a date tonight with Fireman Bob."

"Fireman Bob? Whatever happened to our agreement to go steady? It's been three months with these guys and you're still seeing them!"

I tried to duck out of the question. "Well, I'm sorry, Kai, but it's an assignment!"

"An assignment! Danuta, the assignment was over two months ago. I tried calling my girlfriends back and they won't have anything to do with me. I gave them all up and we saw each other steadily for four days! Now do you call that fair?"

"Well, I can understand how you might feel, but Kai, I can't just call Fireman Bob and cancel a date. It wouldn't be right."

"What does that guy have that I don't have?" he hollered into the phone, exasperated with me. "What do any of those guys give you that I can't give you?"

"Kai, you are my trusted friend and constant companion. They can't hold a candle to you," I tried to reassure him.

"Don't give me that 'trusted friend and constant companion' bit," he said. "I want to be a lot more than that to you." And then he hung up.

Fifteen minutes later the phone rang again. It was Kai.

"What if I were to tell you that in two hours a white Rolls-Royce will be parked out front, waiting to take us to dinner and then dancing, and then will drive us home. You will recognize the car, because the chauffeur will be wearing white gloves and holding two chilled glasses of champagne."

"Kai, I'll call you right back," I chirped.

Seconds later I was on the phone to Fireman Bob.

"Uh, Bob, something's come up and I can't make it tonight."
I hung up and called Kai back.

"Kai, hold the Rolls! I'll be ready by six o'clock sharp."

Poor Kai had to go to extraordinary lengths to get my attention. But he did get it.

And sometimes it cost him. As hostess of a morning television show, I had community obligations to fulfill. One evening the United Way called on me to be Mistress of Ceremonies for an auction to benefit the charity. It was a black-tie affair, and naturally I invited Kai to accompany me, since he was the only man I ever knew who owned his own tuxedo.

Well into the evening, one man in the audience bid five dollars for a kiss from Danuta. Another man joined the fun and bid ten dollars, and quickly someone else bid fifteen. I was a bit embarrassed but I liked it. The bidding sat at fifteen dollars. I looked around the room and saw Kai squirming. He jumped up and, obliging me, yelled, "Twenty dollars!"

"Twenty-two," countered the other bidder.

"Twenty-five," Kai persisted.

"Twenty-seven!" cried the other man.

Heads were swinging from one man to the other as though they were watching a tennis match, and the ball was in Kai's court.

"Thirty-five plus!" hollered Kai. The audience roared with approval, and Kai won the fair maiden's attention one more time.

While I basked in the loving devotion of my best friend, I didn't realize that he was going to Women's Aglow meetings, looking for a Christian wife. He was afraid to talk to me about Jesus, convinced that I would outwit him, outargue him. Jesus was a topic he didn't want to lose me on. His spirit urged him to hold up on that discussion. But he knew it was a discussion we would inevitably have.

Kai was aware of my reputation about marriage. My friends

called me the Anti-Bride. Marriage was anathema to me. It was a condition, an unfamiliar disease of need from which I did not suffer. If an enchanted fellow burst upon me with permanent affections and mentioned marriage, I left skid marks in my dust. That's what happened to the admiral, the chiropractor, the mining engineer, the air force major, the program director, the Buddhist, the tool-and-dye salesman, the parachutist, the tooth ceramicist, my high school steady, the cake baker, the psychologist, and J.J. Kai did not want a Swedish financial consultant added to the list.

I had been invited to many weddings but was only able to endure one and a half ceremonies. The half was because on the way to the wedding, I turned around on the freeway three times trying to avoid the thing, and once there, left early.

I don't think I was being honest with myself about hating marriage. I think I was trying to protect myself from an intense belief that I would never find the kind of happiness to hang my life on as others had. Up to that point my previous relationships were filled with heartbreak and hurts, painful rejections, and deceptions. To believe I could ever have anything other than a temporary involvement would be to admit that I could have something I could not find, that perhaps I was not good enough, or pretty enough, or fast enough, or coy enough, or even capable enough to make such a lifelong commitment. In any case, I was more than mildly defensive. So instead of admitting that love and marriage was painfully unavailable to me, I pretended that I chose not to want it. By now, I think I was believing my own cover-up.

Kai had determined that if he ever married again, it would be to a Christian woman. There was the disturbing conviction that I was what he wanted, but I was someone he couldn't have.

Chapter Six
Meeting the Hound of Heaven

I could not commit myself to Kai. I didn't know the meaning of commitment. I didn't know the meaning of life. That is not to say I led a shallow existence, but rather that I led an existential life based on the belief that my sufferings and critical moments somehow impassioned my reason for living. I believed that life was the sum total of my experiences, and the more I experienced, the more life I had. But if you tried to pin me down and say, "Yes, but what is that life you have more of?" I couldn't answer you. I could only say that I suffered, I sang, and I wanted more.

But I wanted deeper as well. Why was I alive? Why did I rise in the morning? What use was it to brush my teeth and travel down a ribbon of highway to work, struggle and pursue, win and lose, achieve and climb, and then drive home at the end of the day to do it again? What had I to do with the Milky Way? The universe loomed above me, ominous and omnipotent, and I pursued my life on a spinning blue ball, with my heart and soul glued to a massively inconsequential mortality. I couldn't stand the idea that all that was me was so insignificant. An amoeba lives such a life, but not a human being.

And I was bored. I was thirty-three years old and I had it all: a good education, a wonderful career, many friends, plenty of money, a little yellow Porsche, a condominium on the beach, and carte blanche to one of the most beautiful cities in America. What else was there to strive for but more of the same? But more wasn't better, it was just *more*.

I suffered from impermanence. My interests were transient. If I thought I found some answers I could live with one day, I discovered they didn't satisfy the next day. Transcendental Meditation led me to a vacant lot, unoccupied by even my soul. There I sought refuge in hollowness and beauty in a wasteland. Tarot cards, astrology, palmistry—these were my attempts to move myself into the spiritual realm by my own efforts and realize my spirituality by my own power, but my efforts in these areas were never enough. I still didn't feel as if I had plugged into the mother lode.

The argument that all this power is there to be explored and developed didn't make sense to me either. Not until I understood that there are two kingdoms, and both of them work, one for truth and one for deception that utilizes fragments of truth toward its own end of misery, did I see clearly that first one must identify which kingdom one is going to play with, and then be prepared for the consequences if one makes the wrong choice.

I didn't want to *be* god. I wanted to *know* God.

I studied philosophy, thinking if I could understand all the great thoughts of all the great men and women who ever lived, then perhaps I could make a sort of porridge out of it and amalgamate some sense out of this life.

I started a philosophy group with two friends, Ernie and Ron, who had similar questions. Our purpose was to study, analyze, and if possible, refute the arguments of thinkers. We spent hours over bread and wine, pounding out ideas from the likes of Descartes and Nietzsche, Kierkegaard and Hume.

One day Ron brought to the table a book by C. S. Lewis called *Mere Christianity*. That same day I happened to offer to the discussion a book by Friedrich Nietzsche called *The Anti-Christ*. Unknown to us at the time was the fact that we had before us a case for God and a case against God by two of the greatest thinkers of modern times.

When each of us had read both books, we were perplexed by Nietzsche. He appeared to us to be obsessive and angry at a God he refused to recognize. With his fist shaking into the face of God, he insisted that God did not exist. We wondered who he was talking to. For a philosopher with such credentials as Nietzsche to offer emotionalism rather than logic as an argument bothered us:

> "Spirit" is to us precisely a symptom of a relative imperfection of the organism, as an attempting, fumbling blundering, as a toiling in which an unnecessarily large amount of nervous energy is expended—we deny that anything can be made perfect so long as it is still made conscious. "Pure spirit" is pure stupidity; if we deduct the nervous system and the senses, the "mortal frame," we miscalculate—that's all!

We put Nietzsche aside for the time being and picked up on C. S. Lewis.

Lewis was difficult to handle in another way. We couldn't refute him. We found his arguments solid and to our shock, very personal.

Suddenly we were not faced with the intellectual exercise as much as we were faced with our own shaky belief systems:

> I am trying here to prevent anyone saying the really foolish thing that people often say about Him: "I'm ready to accept Jesus as a great moral teacher, but I don't accept His claim to be God." That is the one thing we must not say. A man who was merely a man and said the sort of things Jesus said would not be a great moral teacher. He would either be a lunatic—on a level with the man who says he is a poached egg—or else he would be the Devil of Hell. You must make your choice. Either this man was, and is, the Son of God: or else a madman or something worse. You can shut Him up for a fool, you can spit at Him and kill Him as a demon; or you can fall at His feet and call Him Lord and God. But let us not come with any patronizing nonsense about His being a great human teacher. He has not left that open to us. He did not intend to.

This was a turning point for us. We knew we were reading something vital. It burned through us like only truth can when you come face-to-face with it. We were teetering on an edge and didn't know how to get our balance. Kai came to the rescue.

"I know a philosopher of sorts," he said, "and he knows all about C. S. Lewis. His name is Harald Bredesen, and he lives nearby. Maybe all of you might like to meet him."

That evening the four of us—Ron, Ernie, Kai, and I—marched to Harald's home and met with the suntanned "philosopher." He guided us to a large, round patio table at the back of his house. I could not know what was in store for us that night, but hearts and minds were racing. I became the designated speaker for the group, and hammered away at Harald with every question imaginable.

"Harald, if Jesus Christ really is the Son of God, why didn't He just write in the sky, and say, 'I am He. All who believe in

Me, on this side of the planet. All those who don't, to the other side,' and end the debate? Why two thousand years of progressive redemption and misery for generations?''

"Danuta," Harald started thoughtfully, "do you like to choose your own ice-cream cone at Thirty-one Flavors?''

"What?'' He threw me off track for a moment. "Well, yes, I guess I do. Of course I do,'' I stammered.

"Well, do you think if someone always came along and told you what ice-cream flavor you should have, you'd feel as if you never really got to choose? Would you feel you weren't free, and probably resent that person after a while?''

"Yes, I guess I would.''

"Well, then, God doesn't want you to feel as if you don't have a choice in the matter of your life. He isn't going to tell you to choose Him. He's going to wait until you choose Him on your own, by yourself, out of love, not out of fear or intimidation or threat. Nobody can force anybody to love them, can they?''

I shook my head in agreement.

"I mean, if your mother and father twisted your arm and threatened you unless you loved them, it would be pretty impossible to love them, wouldn't it? Well, God is the same way. He wants you to love Him openly and freely, by your choice. After all, that's the only kind of love that is really love, isn't it?''

"Of course,'' I answered.

"That's why God didn't try to intimidate or force people with a big sign in the sky. He wants you voluntarily, not because it's what everybody else is doing, or because you'll end up in hell. He simply wants you to love Him.''

"Harald,'' I said, trying a different tack, "what happens to people who never hear about Jesus Christ? Are they going to hell?''

"Would you send them to hell?'' Harald countered.

"I certainly would not!" I replied indignantly. "That wouldn't be fair."

"Right!" Harald said. "It wouldn't be fair. Do you believe God is fair?"

"Well, if He's God He has to be fair."

"Then if He is fair, don't you think He would have even more compassion than we mere mortals in the matter?"

"Well, yes, of course." My arguments were getting diffused, one by one.

"Harald, we are all His creatures. Why doesn't He just forgive us all our sins and bring us up to heaven with Him if He wants us with Him, and forego the nasty business of crucifixion, blood, and suffering? Why send Jesus at all?" I was sure I got him on that one.

Harald pulled another question out of thin air. "Danuta, have you ever been stopped for speeding, and given a ticket?"

"Yes, as a matter of fact I have, Harald, but I hardly see what that has to do with. . . ." I felt myself getting impatient with what I believed to be sidetracks to my demands for bottom-line answers.

"What would happen if you went before the judge, and the judge said, 'Danuta, you were speeding fifty miles above the speed limit, but I want you to like me, so I'm going to let you off scot-free.' Would that be justice?" Harald was up to something.

"Of course that wouldn't be *justice*," I emphasized, "but I sure would appreciate it!" I laughed.

"What if that same judge did the same thing for every murderer, liar, thief, sex offender, wife beater, child abuser, adulterer, con artist, embezzler, and all other criminals? Would that be justice? Would that be fair?" Harald was heating up.

"I guess that wouldn't be so good. After all, those people are guilty, and should be punished,'' I said, feeling uncomfortably strident.

"Danuta, God is that judge. And you just admitted that God is perfectly fair. For God to simply overlook the crimes of man and say the law is not important would not be just. Besides, since God is absolute perfection, He could not have anything or anyone with the slightest imperfection around Him or else His absolute perfection wouldn't be so absolute. So God came up with a solution. He would get Someone who would pay the penalty for all those crimes, so that mankind didn't have to pay. The penalty for sin, by the way, is death. But in order to pay the penalty, the One sacrificed in the place of man would have to be perfectly acceptable to God as a sacrifice. Since there is no one perfect enough to be offered up as a sacrificial penitent, God sent His own true and perfect Son to be the sacrificial Lamb. Jesus was the atonement, the sacrifice, and He was innocent."

"But Harald," I interrupted, "how does man benefit from such a plan? What for?"

"Did you ever read *A Tale of Two Cities,* by Charles Dickens?" Harald was at it again, throwing in a wrench out of the clear blue.

"What about *A Tale of Two Cities*?" I asked condescendingly.

"Well, you may remember that in the story one man changed clothes with another and died in his place. Christ has done that for us. Now we are wearing Christ's coat of perfection. The penalty is paid by Him, and we are set free. Now when God looks down upon man, He doesn't see our sins. He sees the blood of Jesus. Now we are acceptable to Him and can come into His presence and be with Him for all eternity."

Silence surrounded us momentarily as we all consumed Harald's words. We had been at it now for over three and a half hours, and it was dark. Harald hadn't offered to put the lights on outside, so there we sat in the darkness, speaking to one another without seeing each other. The others around the table had not spoken in all this time. It was as though whoever won tonight's bout would also win the table of observers.

While digesting the last round of debate, I opened my mouth to fire yet another question at Harald—something about why do good people suffer so much—when a loud male voice interrupted me.

"Your questions are not important."

I didn't recognize the voice that seemed to come from every direction. "Who said that?" I asked.

"Who said what?" asked Kai.

"Who said that my questions were not important?" I was insulted.

"Nobody said any such thing," Ernie said.

"Darling, are you all right?" Kai asked, touching my arm.

I was frozen in thought. *My questions not important, indeed! My questions are everything to me. Without questions I have no answers. Without answers I have no story, and with no story I have no paycheck.* I was a journalist, a reporter, an interviewer. *Questions are everything to me! How dare someone say my questions aren't important!* My internal monologue stopped. And then, as though in an afterthought, in perfect contradiction to the first thoughts came a series of ideas that were not my own, that did not generate from the same well. An inner voice came to me, not from me, and I sat paralyzed, listening.

"If you waited to have all your questions answered to your absolute satisfaction, you would have to wait until you have the mind of God Himself. And that will take a while. If your commitment is predicated on having God's mind, you will never commit to anything, ever. You will never be capable of commitment."

I don't know how long I sat there like that. It could have been hours or seconds, but just then, as though spurred by the Holy Spirit, Harald Bredesen leaped across the table at me, nose-to-nose, and said, "Are you ready to commit to Jesus Christ right now, tonight? Are you willing to have Him in your life?"

Suddenly relieved, as though electricity flowed in my veins, I cried, "Yes!"

Harald stuttered, "You, you, you *are*?" He was flabbergasted.

"You *are*?" Kai said, astonished at my abrupt transformation from cynic to believer.

"You *what*?" asked Ron and Ernie in chorus.

"I would have thought you were the furthest one of us all from saying such a thing," Ernie blurted out in a bewildered laugh.

Harald collected himself from the shock of the century and quickly took advantage of the opening. "Are you all willing to pray tonight and ask that Jesus Christ come into your lives? Are you all willing to wear His coat of perfection?"

We all became deadly serious and nodded.

"Then pray this prayer out loud with me," Harald began.

"Lord Jesus, I believe You are the Son of God. I believe You died on the cross for my sins. I am a sinner, God. And I'm sorry for sinning against you. Forgive me now. Lord Jesus, I ask You to come into my heart. Be Lord and Master of my life. Come live Your life in me, and I will serve You all the rest of my days. In Jesus' name. Amen."

We sat there, mesmerized at the profundity of what we had just done. No one spoke for several minutes. I began to giggle. "Yea!" I cheered. "Hooray!" I didn't know the official terminology was "Alleluia."

"Yeah, that's all right," bubbled Ernie. This was the first time I had seen him smile in months.

"I love you, Danuta," Kai said, putting his arms around me and kissing me on the cheek.

"Oh, Kai, I'm so happy!" I squealed.

That night we went home in a fit of giggles and laughter, as though we had all been drinking. We knew something wonderful had happened, but we weren't quite sure we understood it all yet. But we were about to learn. Harald quickly put us in touch with a biblical scholar named Coleman Phillips, pastor of Cathedral of the Valley Church in Escondido, California. The philosophy group became a Bible-study group. Coleman sat with us every Tuesday night in Ernie's house and fought the good fight. We weren't easy on him.

We were not your typical Bible students. We were belligerent, arrogant, hostile, and deadly practical. We hated dogma and always wanted proof. We were not willing to accept anything by faith if we didn't have to. We had already put our intellect aside and accepted Christ through faith. Now our minds demanded the intellectual satisfaction of our decision. We needed to harmonize heart and brain.

Years later Coleman admitted that every Tuesday night before this Bible class his prayer was, "Oh, God, do I have to?"

"Coleman!" I charged, one night, "Why don't I just finish it all off right here, right now? What's the use of going on?"

"Whaa, what?" Coleman looked stunned.

"I mean, why in the world do I have to keep on living? I'm not doing any good where I am. Jesus saved me. I accept. So now let's get on with it. Why not suicide and heaven!" I was serious.

"You just can't ice yourself off," Ernie interjected.

"And why not? Where in the Bible does it say that suicide is illegal?" I challenged.

"Danuta, God has a plan for all of us. He wants us to know that plan and live according to it. If there were no good reason for being here outside of salvation, I suppose God would call us home the second we got saved.''

"Humph. That makes sense," I admitted. "So, Coleman, what are we studying tonight?" And so it went, for the next two years.

During my first year as a newborn Christian, a series of unusual things happened to me that seemed to be preparing me for something big. Little did I dream just how big, *big* was!

A few weeks after accepting Christ I was offered a free trip to Israel. I had been in Jerusalem for one day when I received a phone call from the former head of the Jerusalem bureau for *Time* magazine, David Aikman. David had heard about me from Harald Bredesen, and he invited me to a Bible-study meeting in the home of Menachem Begin.

The meeting drew some thirty rabbis and scholars from Jerusalem and Tel Aviv. I was the only blond in the bunch. And I was thrilled to the bone to be there, in the prime minister's house, listening to his ideas of a God I had just met. When the meeting ended, Begin was being hustled upstairs to bed, while saying goodnight to the group at the same time. It was my only chance to introduce myself. I tried getting his attention by tapping on his shoulder from behind, while all thirty were in front of him.

"Mr. Prime Minister, sir, uh, excuse me, Mr. Prime Minister!" It was no use. I might as well have been a little bird chiseling on the Rock of Gibraltar. Just then a verse from Ephesians jumped out at me: ''. . . having done all, to stand. Stand therefore . . . (Ephesians 6:13, 14). At the time, this was crazy, because I had never read Ephesians. I hardly realized there was an Old Testament and a New Testament, much less the separate letters of Paul! But those words moved me into action.

I sought out an adjacent corner of the room and stood there as still as I could, with my eyes boring into the crowd. Everyone was shaloming everyone else, and I watched as the prime minister was being shalomed right out the door. And then something extraordinary happened. He looked up and saw me. He was quickly led back into the crowd of well-wishers when he glanced back and saw me again. By the third time he couldn't take it anymore. He parted the crowd before him as though they were the Red Sea, strode across the room with his hand extended to me, and said, "Shalom, my name is Menachem Begin. And who are you?"

I forgot who I was. He was shaking my hand and introducing himself to me! I couldn't believe my eyes! Now, I am not one to be tongue-tied. After all, I interviewed Ben Hur, Moses, and El Cid all in one shot. Charlton Heston was my hero, and I wasn't half as nervous at that moment as I was right now. And I still couldn't get my voice back.

Finally David appeared at my side. "Mr. Prime Minister, this is Danuta Rylko. She's a journalist from San Diego."

"Ah," Begin said, "and why are you here?"

"Well, I'm here because, well, I don't know why I'm here
. . ." I said, with a great deal of sophistication.

"Danuta is here to do an interview with you," David offered.

I shot David a quick glance. I was?

"One day, young lady, you will be interviewing leaders from all around the world. One day. . . ." And with that, Begin exited the room, leaving me gasping for breath and trying to understand what had just happened.

Upon my return to San Diego, I couldn't fathom how I was supposed to be interviewing world leaders. After all, I was living in San Diego, doing a morning talk show. How would I get to be such a privileged interviewer?

Months later, lying on the sand in front of my condominium, a stranger came up to me and said her husband had had a dream about me.

"My husband never dreams, and even if he does dream," she said, "why should he dream about you?"

I assured her I didn't know her husband.

"The dream is that he's climbing a staircase to see a great rabbi. We're Jewish, you know," she said. "Anyway, my husband is expecting to see this rabbi at the top of the stairs, but instead of a rabbi standing there, you are standing there. What does it mean?"

I didn't know what it meant, but she seemed so insistent for some interpretation of this dream that it stayed with me for a few days. Then two days later, my Jewish co-host on "Sun Up" said to me, "Hey, I had a dream about you last night. Funny thing is, I don't dream, and even if I do, I never remember my dreams. But this dream was that you were on a national television show for Jesus Christ."

"Oh, no," I moaned, "not another Jewish dream!"

The following afternoon, Harald called me and we went for a walk on the beach. I told him about the dreams, and wondered what they meant. Harald stopped dead in his tracks, put his hand on my shoulder, and said, "It is confirmed in my spirit that you are to send a videotape of your work to CBN, and a letter with the dreams in it."

CBN was unknown to me at the time, because the "700 Club" and my show competed for the same time slot on different channels. Besides, I had never sent a letter with dreams in it to prospective employers in all my life. But for some reason, I decided to honor Harald's wishes and sent the information off. Nothing happened. I forgot about it.

Nine months later I received a call from CBN. I thought the

man on the other end of the line said CBS. He identified himself as the executive producer for CBN, and said he had just seen my tape.

"What tape?" I asked.

"The tape you sent us nine months ago," he said apologetically. "You see, we were cleaning out an old desk, and just happened to come across a letter that was still sealed, and a videotape that no one has looked at until now. And I believe you're the woman we've been looking for."

"For what?" I asked.

"For the '700 Club,' " he answered.

"Yes," I said, "but what's the name of the show?"

I auditioned as a guest co-host on the program for one day, then flew back to San Diego and waited on their decision. Pat Robertson told Harald I was "sweet." I have never been called "sweet" in my entire life. Ben Kinchlow said I was "nice." That's another word I hate.

But my hopes were high. I felt that something was happening. After the first week, having heard nothing from CBN, I began to get discouraged. More than that, I was mad. And I was going to tell God just how mad I was. I really was going to let Him have it.

I walked out on to the beach and started walking up and down the shoreline, screaming my rage into the sky. "Enough! Do You hear me up there? I say enough! I don't want any more of Your hope! If You can't come through on Your promises, then don't dangle hope in my face. I can't take any more of it! I am sick and tired of Your dreams and visions and prophecies—all of it. Just leave me alone. And take Your hope away from me!" I fell to the sand, exhausted, and cried my heart out.

Suddenly there was a gust of sweet scented wind, as though someone with fine perfume had just walked up behind me. I turned and saw no one there, but the perfumed air remained. As nostalgically as the scent of new-mowed grass or just-baked cookies brings one back to a picture of another time and place, this perfume said to me, "Jerusalem."

I looked into the sky and it seemed as though the clouds had absorbed land and sea, and I was at once swallowed up into the belly of God. I saw heaven. And these words creased into my brain: "The doors are now open to you. Have faith in God."

The Bible says God hears the fervent prayers of a righteous man. He heard mine. I was crying, "Oh, thank You, God. Thank You, thank You," when I entered my condo. The phone was ringing.

"Danuta, this is Kai. I just wanted you to know that I've been impressed to tell you that you have that job at CBN."

"I know!" I shouted into the phone. "I know!"

The next day, CBN called. I had the job.

Two weeks later, on my birthday, February 22, 1983, I quit my television show, my afternoon radio broadcasts, my motivational program for teenagers, and my swim school for babies. I packed up my old cat and a suitcase, said good-bye to my church, Coleman, the Bible study, my family, my boyfriend, and Kai, and drove across the country to do God only knew what.

Left: Talking with two
of my favorite guests
on the "700 Club,"
Gavin and Patti
MacLeod.

Center Left: News on
"Sun Up, San Diego."

Center Right: In 1982,
as a young reporter,
I had a surprising
encounter with
Menachem Begin at a
Bible study held in his
home in Jerusalem.

Below Left: On the set at the "700 Club":
Ben Kinchlow, me, and Pat Robertson.

Below Right: Learning to handle a mini-cam at
the University of Colorado, 1970.

Inset: Wet and wild ... shooting the rapids of the Gauley River with Kai, 1986. We are the two people in the front! All you can see of Kai is his helmet.

From river canyons to mountaintops, I believe in living life with a passion, to the fullest. Switzerland, 1975.

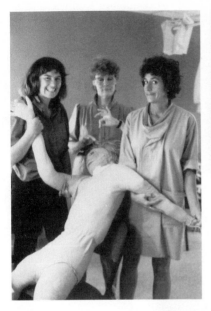

Left: In the bridal dressing room with friends Suzanne Shannon, Olivia Teja, and Michelle Theriot. I am not the limp, frightened bride in the middle. I took the picture ... as well as the kidding. San Diego, 1983.
Above: A formally attired Harald Bredesen, toasting us after the wedding.

Finally ....

My best friend, Kai.

Above: Me, pumpkin, and Solomon, at home on the Wild Kingdom in Virginia.

Right: My country-and-western Swede. Kai is a financial adviser, but he has also rediscovered a singing career in a ministry of music.

Below: Marriage means having your best friend by your side all the time.

Chapter Seven
The Wind Chimes

I was hired as an international correspondent, but in the meantime, I found myself the temporary co-host of the "700 Club." Three weeks after arriving at the center, a memo came across my desk addressed to the entire staff:

"I don't care if it is just a two-man-show format, change the format to a three-person show. From now on Danuta Rylko will be a regular co-host on the '700 Club.' Make all necessary changes. [Signed] Pat."

That's how I found out I was a permanent fixture on the "700 Club." Any discussion about my future as an international correspondent simply wasn't brought up. The position as co-host felt natural and easy, and Terry Heaton, the producer, Pat, Ben, Michael Little, the executive producer, and I all came to the same unspoken agreement: this was what I had come to CBN to do. I don't even recall anyone saying congratulations! It was as though I had always been there. Sort of.

My comfort with Pat and Ben was exceeded only by my remarkable naivete. It was almost two months before the weight of my undertaking began to take effect. I started hearing things like, "Do you realize you are one of the most visible representatives of Christian women in all of Christendom?" Who, me, who had known the Lord for all of two years? Then someone would quote statistics such as, "Are you aware that more people watch the '700 Club' every week than read all the news magazines and newspapers, including *Time, Newsweek,* the *Wall Street Journal,* and the *New York Times* combined?" Or they would say, "The '700 Club' is viewed in thirty-three million households, fifteen thousand communities, and forty-six countries!" Suddenly it was dawning on me, this was no ordinary television program! I was representing the love and sacrifice of Christ, and I was standing between two spiritual giants: Pat Robertson and Ben Kinchlow! Little old me started feeling smaller and smaller. I became unsure of myself, afraid of making a blunder on the air, afraid of not appearing spiritual enough, afraid I had bitten off more than I could chew. Each day I found myself praying in my car on my way to work, "Oh, God, don't let them know You've made a mistake here. Don't let them know who I really am. Don't let them find out I'm not anybody special. Above all, dear Lord, don't blow my cover!"

My discomfort began to take on signs of physical distress. I became quiet. Pat and Ben would chat about things on the set and I would sit there, smiling and mute. This situation existed for several weeks before it caught the attention of Bob Slosser, then CBN News Director. He called me into his office one day as I was waiting for the elevator, and with a hearty, warm smile he said, "You know, Danuta, we hired you because of who you are, what you are, and how you are. Don't be afraid of being yourself. That's why we love you! That's why the Holy Spirit sent you here. I think you should let it all hang out and just go for it!''

"Just go for it?" I stammered. "What if I say something somebody doesn't like? What happens then?''

"Oh, sure," he said. "There will be days when you find yourself getting slapped up the side of the head, figuratively speaking, for going too far, or going beyond the limits, but the risk is worth it. You'll be you.''

"So, when I step out of bounds, I can just point my finger at you and say, 'Bob told me I could'?" I laughed with gusto for the first time in weeks.

"Well, yes, I guess you can." Bob stood up and gave me a big hug. "So just go for it, kiddo.''

I walked out of his office feeling elated, light, free, and approved of. Since that time I have never again felt intimidated or ashamed of being who I am. I realize that we who serve the Lord are all ordinary people with extraordinary grace, whether we are on television or plowing a field of corn or nursing a baby.

It was during these transitional months at CBN that I began to feel isolated from my friends and family in San Diego. I felt lonely and grew homesick for the blue Pacific and the dolphins that dance in the surf. I missed Mexican food, mariachi bands, bougainvilleas, outdoor restaurants, the informality of life, palm trees, and the dry Santa Ana winds that blow in from the desert. I had left all the things I loved, and all the people I loved, for this calling from Christ. My spirit told me that what I had done was right, but my bones ached for home.

One day I received a phone call from Harald.

"Uh, Danuta, you are my daughter in the Lord, aren't you?'' Harald asked in a way that led me to believe he had something up his sleeve.

"Yes, of course I am, Harald!" It was so good to hear a familiar voice.

"Well, then, you know, Danuta, that a woman of your age ought to be thinking of something a little more permanent."

"You mean like death, Harald? You mean a will?" I didn't think a woman of my age was all that old. After all, I was only thirty-four and felt as if I was just getting into my stride as a woman.

"Oh no, no, no, not death!" Harald chuckled. "I mean marriage!"

"Marriage? Marriage! What do you mean, *marriage*?" By now the thought of a will was more palatable.

"Well, now," Harald began to speak more quickly, sensing he was losing his case before he had even begun. "I was just thinking that since you are my daughter in the Lord, that wonderful fellow Kai Soderman would make a terrific son-in-law!" There, he had managed to get it all out. He listened to the silence crackling over the long-distance lines.

"Uh, Danuta, are you still there?"

"Harald," I said, struggling for composure, "marriage is a very heavy thing, and it's great that you think Kai is the right man for me, but I don't think I can marry Kai, because after all, Harald, marriage is a very serious business. I love Kai like a brother, I mean, he's my best friend, but to marry him, well, I'd have to be in love with him, wouldn't I, and I'm not in love with him, but I do love him, very much, you know what I mean, Harald?"

"Yeeees," Harald dragged that little word out so slowly that I knew he was thinking of something. I was afraid to ask what. "We'll have to pray about this, won't we," he finally said.

Relieved to hear him dropping the subject, I said something

like, "Thank you for calling and thinking of me, Harald," and gratefully hung up.

But that wasn't to be the end of it as far as Harald was concerned. He quickly called Kai.

"Uh, hello, Kai? Boy, do I have plans for you!" He blurted into the phone.

Kai and Harald agreed to meet in a Taco Bell parking lot, and instead of going in to eat as Kai had expected, they marched up and down the parking lot for two hours praying in tongues, praising the Lord, hugging each other, and talking about the possibilities of a Kai-and-Danuta marriage.

Finally Kai said, "Harald, I love Danuta with all my heart. I'd do absolutely anything in the world for her. I would love to marry that woman. But she's not in love with me, and there's no way I can influence her in the matter. Believe me, I've tried!"

Harald stopped walking and faced Kai. "Kai, when things get tough like this, make it as difficult on God as you possibly can and make it as easy on yourself as you can."

"In that case, Harald," Kai said, "let's pray that Danuta will propose to me!"

And so the deal was made.

One week later Kai called me to say he was coming for a visit. Something told me this wasn't just a social call. I knew Kai was going to propose to me, and I would have to tell my best friend that I could not marry him. It was a conversation I was not looking forward to having.

I tried to avoid the inevitable serious moment. The day he arrived I made a dozen excuses for why we always had to be in a crowd of people. From the corner of my eye I saw Kai watching me, like a *Mona Lisa* whose eyes followed me around the room, smiling at every nervous little laugh and fluttering gesture, reading my precious fears like a morning newspaper, eyes that loved me with a steady, clear gaze, filled with secrets, inescapable.

My careful orchestration lapsed, and suddenly we were alone in my dressing room at the "700 Club."

"Darling," was all he whispered, slowly walking toward me.

I jumped at the sound of his voice, as though a cannon had just been fired next to my ear, and unconsciously took a few faltering steps backwards.

"Darling, it's only fair that you should know I think you and I ought to be married." He said it so softly, so certainly, with a slight hint of amusement in his voice, as he watched my reaction.

I opened my mouth to protest the very idea, but he raised his hand to stop me.

"This is not a proposal. And I don't want your answer. I want the answer that God gives you."

What a relief! I was off the hook. He didn't want my answer! Now I could pray, hear from God, and then tell him no!

So, dutifully, I bowed my head, holding Kai's hands, and we asked God for divine guidance in this matter. Little did I know how God was about to tangle with my heart.

Kai had arranged a romantic dinner for two in a quaint little restaurant called Three Ships Inn, in Virginia Beach. We sat next to a fireplace merrily crackling with logs, and apprehensively I blinked at Kai over the candlelight. Kai took a deep breath and went into gear, laying out our possible future.

"Naturally, I'll move to Virginia Beach, since I don't think you are prepared to leave CBN," he concluded, waiting for a positive reaction.

"Will it be difficult for you to relocate your business?" I asked.

"No, not at all," he replied. "That's the beauty of it all. As long as I have a telephone and my business contacts, I can conduct investment counseling anywhere in the world."

"How much money did you make last year?" I started interviewing him.

"Well, I made—" The waitress interrupted with the main course, and cleared Kai's untouched salad plate and soup bowl. I was eating my stuffed flounder, listening to Kai plead his case for a stable and secure future, while his food turned cold on his plate.

"So how much money do you expect to be making within the next five years?" I wasn't holding anything back. If I was going to even *think* about marriage, it was going to be in cold, practical, rational terms. Too many times I had heard my friends tell me love goes out the window when you can't pay the rent. I was not going to let that happen to me, even though I knew that would be an unthinkable situation with Kai.

Kai swallowed hard several times during the interrogation, but he answered all my questions head-on, as though he was prepared for the grilling. He built little castles out of the Sweet 'N Low and sugar packets, and meticulously lined up his knife, spoon, and fork with his napkin. While he spoke he absentmindedly reshuffled his water glass with the salt and pepper shakers, and then readjusted the knife and spoon with his napkin.

"Kai, you realize that if we get married, I won't be the ordinary, everyday kind of wife, don't you? I mean, if we get married, you probably won't have dinner on the table every night at a precise hour. I don't believe that a wife has to be the maid just because she's a woman."

"Absolutely, darling. I couldn't agree with you more about that," Kai jumped in enthusiastically. "If I wanted just an ordinary wife, I wouldn't be suggesting marriage with you. Besides, I don't want a *wife,* I want *you,* just the way you are."

Kai was agreeing with me. I tried to discourage him in another way. "I work best with my mind and my creativity, and sometimes I don't want to do housework. I keep a clean and tidy home, mind you, but if we were married, I wouldn't be running behind you picking up things. I expect an equal amount of help in the kitchen and around the house from you.''

"Absolutely. Absolutely. In fact, darling, I'd insist that we have a housekeeper come in every day.''

"Well, I'm not that untidy!'' I laughed.

"How about every other day?'' Kai volunteered with a smile.

"About children. I want some,'' I said quietly.

The Sweet 'N Low castle fell over. "Children. Fine. We can have children. How many children were you thinking of?'' I sensed Kai faltering on this one. After all, the poor man already had eight!

"I don't know how many children. But I'd like to know we have the option of having children if we want them. Do you have any problem with that?''

"No. No problem. I'll have my vasectomy reversed. They're doing it all the time now, you know.'' He picked up the water glass with his right hand and put it down with his left hand.

"And if we have children,'' I pressed on, "I'll need some help with them. Maybe a nanny.''

"Of course, all the help you need. That's a deal.''

The waitress reappeared and scooped away Kai's untouched meal. "You don't like the food?'' she asked.

"Food, yes, fine, wonderful food, but not right now. I'm very busy here.''

I was working him hard. We talked about vacation spots and honeymoons. Pastimes and pets. Laundry and exercise. And who was going to do the grocery shopping. I finished with my list. Kai won the round that night. He had all his ducks in a row, and had a ready answer for each question. He had obviously been thinking about this for a long time.

And then Kai informed me that he was leaving for New York on a business trip and would be back in exactly one week.

"Not necessarily for an answer. Don't feel pressured."

"Sure," I said, smiling sickly.

He tried to comfort me, but I wasn't in the mood for being comforted. I was in the mood for being scared out of my socks.

Kai followed the Scripture that advises we are to let the peace of God be our umpire, and to have no mind of our own in the matter. He left for New York, serene, secure in the peace of Christ that we would indeed be married.

That week was the longest week of my life. Kai may have had no mind of his own in the matter, but I had no mind of my own at all! I'm not usually one to not have an opinion about something. I always have an opinion on things, and if by some miracle I have no opinion, I'll make one up! But not this time. I had no opinion about anything. I could not decide what to wear in the morning, trying on three and four outfits for the day. I couldn't decide where to go for lunch, pulling into a restaurant parking lot and pulling out again, unable to make up my mind where to eat, or if I was fortunate enough to get inside an establishment, I couldn't decide *what* to eat! During the entire week, I was in absolute neutral. It was as if God put me there on purpose, knowing I wouldn't be willing to go there on my own.

I ran into a used-car salesman that week who convinced me to buy a huge, black 1979 Pontiac Bonneville with a leaky radiator, without a working air conditioner. And I already owned a perfectly good car!

I was in such a tizzy that I almost expected Pat and Ben to rebuke the spirit of weirdness in me. Terry Heaton, the producer, took me behind one of the sets at the "700 Club" one day to pray for me. I was panicking.

Monday night I found myself unable to sleep, tossing in bed, trying to come up with some way of knowing how I felt about Kai and me and marriage and life in general. I turned to my bedside clock and the ubiquitous green digits that tell you the time, whether you want to know it or not, flashed out at me: 12:03 A.M.

I looked up at the ceiling and gazed at the wind chimes hanging beside my bed. I remembered how my philosophy turned Bible-study group had given me those wind chimes for my birthday the year before. They were made of six two-foot-long copper tubes, and I had put them in my bedroom for decorative purposes. In California, the only time they rang was during earthquakes.

Living on the sixteenth floor of a high-rise building, the smallest rumble could set the chimes off, since the top of a tall building sways more radically than the bottom floors. I considered them my own personal nighttime earthquake alarm system since, by the time I heard the first few tinkles of the chimes, I would be awake. Then, as the intensity of the quake increased, the chimes would be clanging, the cupboard doors would be slapping open and shut, and hanging baskets of flowers would swing wildly in the dark. My wind chimes served to forewarn me of possible impending doom. It seemed appropriate this night for the wind chimes to ring their little clangers off. I certainly was sensing impending doom.

But there they hung, dull and stupid, a cold, primitive metal ignorant of my pain, oblivious to my anxiety, merrily waiting for a hurricane or an earthquake or another act of God to move them to action.

An act of God. That's exactly what I needed. The Bible tells the story of Gideon putting out a fleece for a sign from God. Gideon asked God for an answer and proposed that the answer would come through a series of signs involving the sheepskin. A private communication just between God and Gideon. And God had spoken to Gideon through signs with the fleece. Well, I figured, God can speak to me, too! So I put out my own fleece in a prayer.

"Lord, if You want me to marry Kai, make these wind chimes ring, as a sign between You and me." I held my breath and waited. And waited. And waited. I must have waited two or three minutes, and quickly getting discouraged when nothing happened, I muttered something about my stupidity for putting my life in the tinkle of wind chimes, rolled over, and tried to sleep. This was going to be harder than I thought. This was something I had to drive through myself. This wasn't the kind of question one leaves to ambiguous feelings and silly signs. We were talking about life and death here—we were talking about *marriage!*

Tuesday. Wednesday. Pontiac Thursday. Friday. Saturday was coming, and I still had no idea what kind of an answer God was giving me. I felt abandoned, with the most important decision of my life before me.

Friday night I slept in a fever. I woke up unable to breathe. My heart was flapping wildly in my chest. I was choking, awash in perspiration from my head to my toes. I glanced at the clock: 12:03 A.M. it proclaimed. There was something familiar in that. I squeezed my eyes shut, trying to concentrate. What was happening to me? I felt as if my whole life had been turned upside down. Why was I acting so neurotic? Why couldn't I think? Why couldn't I sleep? Why had I suddenly turned into a bumbling turnip?

And then something quite remarkable happened. I found myself whispering, "Oh, God, am I falling in love with Kai?" I surprised myself with that idea, but it felt curiously warm and satisfying to say it. "I am in love with Kai! I am completely and absolutely head over heels in love with Kai!" I was shouting out the words just to hear myself finally say them. I started giggling. "I'm in love with Kai!" I was lying on my back in bed with a grin from ear to ear. I had just been hit with a revelation. *I was in love with Kai.*

The impact of this sudden giddy feeling had stunned me so that I didn't immediately notice the clamoring going on at my bed-side. I couldn't believe what I was hearing—the wind chimes were ringing!

I threw back the covers on the bed and sprang to my feet. "Oh, my God!" I screamed. "It's an earthquake!" Instinctively I braced my feet, grabbed hold of the bedpost, and waited for the ground to thunder. After several seconds, I realized the floor was not moving, my hanging plants were not swaying, and the cup-boards were not slamming open and shut. It took a few more seconds to become aware of the overlooked fact that this was Virginia Beach, Virginia. They don't have earthquakes here. I checked the windows; they were closed. There was no fan, no air conditioner. There I stood in the still, dark night, in the middle of my bedroom, my eyes wide and unbelieving, watching the wind chimes ringing of their own volition, for no earthly reason.

It was then I remembered I had put out a fleece. I had asked God Almighty for a private line, a sign just between Him and me. I wanted the wind chimes to ring if I was to marry Kai, and because God didn't jump at my command, I thought He had forgotten me. But in a dramatic play, the Lord waited until I knew I loved Kai from the inside before He confirmed it on the outside.

And confirm it He did. The wind chimes were not just tinkling, they were clanging and banging and bashing into one another, in the fashion of the grand finale to the *1812 Overture*. It was as if God Himself was leaning over from His high and holy throne in heaven, playing an extraterrestrial tune on my chimes, just to get my attention.

I slept soundly for the first time all week. The next morning I woke up like the model in a Posturepedic mattress commercial. I tossed back the covers and bounced out of bed. I was still grinning. I felt as if it were my birthday, as if sublime and surprising events were about to occur. The world took on surrealistic overtones, as though I were seeing everything through a wide-angle lens; common household items loomed larger than life and held my attention for long seconds at a time. I found myself daydreaming through my cereal with a fork, and stabbing at a raisin left floating in the milky puddle at the bottom of the bowl. I was in love, and I was meeting him at noon for lunch.

"Oh, Kai! I love you!" I gushed when I saw him.

He very nearly patted me on the head. "And I love you, too," he said.

He obviously wasn't getting the full throttle of my meaning. "I don't mean like a friend, Kai. I mean I really love you!" I threw my arms around his neck and pulsed my eyebrows a couple of times at him.

"What?" he said in disbelief.

"Kai! For heaven's sake," I shouted, "last night the Lord rang my chimes!"

Kai had never heard that expression before, but something told him this was good news.

He swooped me off my feet, whirled me around the room, and planted a heavenly kiss on my lips. The arrows of love had definitely hit their target.

I was dazed and wobbling, my knees were weak. I called my mother.

"Mom, oh, Mom, you'll never guess in a million years what happened! Kai is here and—"

"And you're going to get married!" Mom completed the sentence.

"Well, that's what I don't know. Last night I heard the wind chimes ring, and God answered my prayer and now I love Kai with all my heart, but what am I going to do now?" I was babbling.

"Well," she calmly replied, "what *are* you going to do now?"

"I know." I tried to be the sophisticated, educated woman I thought I was, although I was beginning to have my doubts. "I'm going to wait two weeks, and at the end of two weeks, I'll give him my answer."

Mothers have a way of getting to the bottom line real fast, and my mother is no exception. "Two weeks! Two weeks!" she hollered into the phone. "You've known the man for six years! What's two more weeks going to tell you except that you are a coward!"

Now that was a low blow. I had been an amateur race-car driver, a sky diver, a scuba diver, a ski instructor, a swim instructor, and no one could call me a coward, not even my mother!

"Oh, yeah?" I said into the phone. "We'll see about that!"

I hung up the phone and went into the garage, where Kai was looking at the Pontiac, shaking his head. He couldn't believe I had bought the thing.

"Mr. Soderman?" I called, above the hood of the car.

"Yes, darling?" He smiled back.

"Mr. Soderman," I mustered up my nerve. "Mr. Soderman, will you marry me?"

And Kai remembered the prayer in the Taco Bell parking lot with Harald Bredesen: that I would propose to him. Six weeks later, on October 8, 1983, we were married in the Old Globe Theatre in San Diego. Harald was best man.

And the wedding invitation read:

Mrs. John Rylko
requests the honour of your presence
at the marriage (finally!) of her daughter
Danuta

to

Mr. Kai H.R. Soderman
on Saturday, the eighth of October
nineteen hundred and eighty-three
at three o'clock
Festival Stage
Old Globe Theatre
Balboa Park
San Diego, California
Reception immediately following

Chapter Eight
Together at Last

The Wedding

*T*hree days before we were married, I was sick as a dog. I couldn't lift my head off the pillow. I lost my voice and could not even whisper without a furious coughing spasm. If it were not for my mother's homemade chicken noodle soup four times a day, I would never have made it down the aisle. I don't think I was as sick as I was anxious. It's not that I didn't want to marry Kai, and it's not that I wasn't absolutely positive that I was deeply and irrevocably in love with the most complete man I had ever known; it was just that the Anti-Bride part of me wasn't going down without a fight.

It had always been my dream that if I ever did have a wedding, I would be married outside under the sun, with a light breeze tugging at my veil. But I wasn't planning on a hurricane. The morning of October 8, a hurricane watch was in effect, complete with rain and gale-force winds. The ceremony was to take place on an outdoor Shakespearean stage in Balboa Park. I was certain that the clouds would dry up before three o'clock and the sun would shine, just as I figured it should.

At eleven o'clock Kai called. "My darling, it doesn't look as if the sky will clear up today. We may have to move the wedding indoors to the Old Globe Theatre."

"Oh, no!" I whined. "Don't do that, Kai. The weather will clear up, I'm sure of it! I want to be married outside."

"Well, okay," he said, not sounding at all convinced. "We'll wait another hour, but we'll have to make a decision by then, because we've got an orchestra waiting to set up, and I don't think they're too enthusiastic about getting the grand piano wet. Besides, we have two hundred fifty people coming who have to be redirected indoors if we change plans."

"Oh, don't worry," I reassured him. "Honestly, this weather will clear up, it always does. You know it never rains in Southern California!" I hung up, persuaded that all would be fine. Well, it wasn't. An hour later Kai called back, determined.

"Danuta, I've made the decision. We're moving indoors."

"What? We're moving? No way!" I bellowed indignantly.

"Danuta, someone has to make a decision about this, and I have made it. The orchestra leader is refusing to set up and the lead guitarist is afraid of being electrocuted. I've told everybody to set up inside."

"Kai, I don't care about any of that. We'll mop up the stage if there's a little drizzle on it. I want to get married outdoors." I wasn't going to budge an inch.

"All right, then," Kai said rather solemnly. "If that's the way you want it."

"That's the way I want it." And then, as if to soften my

inflexibility and pacify the groom, I said almost apologetically, "I love you, Kai."

"I love you too, Danuta." He hung up first.

I didn't like that phone call. I didn't like the way I sounded. Kai had made a decision and I revoked it. *Some submissive wife-to-be*, I thought. "I veto the first decision Kai makes on our wedding day. Brother!" I muttered under my breath. And then I looked out the window. The winds were bending the palm trees over and rain was driving up against the windowpane.

I called Kai back. "Kai? Hi. It's me, your almost-a-wife? Listen, I think I really got out of line a few minutes ago. I mean, you made the decision to a change of venue, and I should have submitted to that decision, and I didn't. I'm really sorry. Go ahead and call everybody back and tell them we'll move indoors after all."

"I don't have to call them back. They're already setting up indoors." Kai was chuckling.

"You mean you didn't change the plans when I asked you to?"

"Nope."

I smiled self-consciously. I remembered what my pastor, Coleman Phillips, had told me a few days before: "Danuta, I think Kai is the only man in the world who can handle being married to you."

That afternoon, on my way to the theatre, I looked out the window of the car and said rather wistfully to my bridesmaids, "Just think, this is the last time I'll ever take a car ride as a single woman." A few minutes later we stopped at a 7-11 for some blond hairpins that we had forgotten and I said, "Just think, this is the last time I'll ever stop at a Seven-Eleven as a single person." Five minutes later, driving down the freeway, a square-jawed blond right out of *Gentlemen's Quarterly* whizzed by us driving a yellow Mercedes convertible. He turned his head and smiled at me as he sailed by. "Just think," I said nostalgically, "this is the last time I'll ever get to flirt with a hunk in a yellow Mercedes." So I smiled back.

An hour before Kai and I were married, my good friend and hairdresser from CBN, Olivia Teja, was fooling with my hair, cooing calmly in my ear, while my former "700 Club" makeup artist, Linda Enos, was cracking jokes while dabbing me with a powder puff. My mother, glowing with excitement, was poking pink roses into jumbo batches of baby's breath, readying the bridesmaids' bouquets at the last minute. Jackie Mitchum, the "700 Club" guest-services coordinator, was coordinating the guests. I was in the dressing room hyperventilating.

Meanwhile, Kai was quietly rehearsing his wedding vows in the next room with my brother Michael. He was unruffled and reflective. A soft ambience enfolded him like a velvety dream, punctuated by the subdued baritones of the contingency around him.

In my nervousness, I had managed to put my gown on inside out. My dearest friends, Suzanne Shannon and Michelle Theriot, were helping me to redress. Michelle helped me balance as Suzanne guided my feet into my gown and then into my shoes. Then we discovered that someone had locked Olivia's dress in another room, where it was supposed to be ironed, and nobody could find the key. Olivia and Linda had come all the way from Virginia Beach to be with me on this day. I was not about to get married without them. Everyone scrambled, looking for the lost key, while Olivia stood shivering in her slip, giving me a final touch-up on my hair and adjusting my veil for the fourteenth time, waiting for her clothes. Twenty minutes later, the key was found, Olivia was dressed, and I was ready at last. I sat staring at myself in the mirror, feeling like a contender for the heavyweight boxing championship of the world, preparing for that walk into the ring.

Someone handed me my bouquet. I turned in a daze and headed for the door, floated up six steps to the entrance of the theatre at the top of the aisle, and stood in the shadows. I listened to Kai, choking back his tears, singing to me from the altar:

> Now I take you as my bride,
> To always keep you by my side.
> The years will come,
> The years will go,
> God shares our love,
> He told you so.

I was shaking so hard my bouquet was a blur in my hands. I don't know when I stopped breathing, but my body was going into oxygen depletion. I was getting dizzy and I began swaying backwards. Sally, Kai's oldest daughter, was behind me, whispering, "Just give it to the Lord, Dee. Just give it to the Lord."

The orchestra started playing my tune, "Here Comes the Bride," and I walked toward my eldest brother, Richard, who gave me his arm and escorted me a third of the way down the aisle to my brother Michael, who escorted me to Paul, the youngest, who delivered me to Kai. When I reached Kai's side he put his strong arm around my waist and helped hold me up. I took my first deep breath, and blinked. This was really happening.

Kai was looking at me with a tenderness I have never seen in the face of another human being. "Danuta, I have always loved you, from the very first day I met you." He was speaking boldly, for all the world to hear. "I promise to be the husband you need, the husband you can always depend on, and the husband who will always encourage a closer walk with our Lord Jesus Christ."

It was my turn. "Kai, I have always loved you. I have turned from all others, and give you my heart, my hopes, and my life. You have my pledge on this."

We shared communion, and then Harald called a blessing upon us with a thunderous "Alleluia!" slapping us on our shoulders with enthusiasm that nearly punched us down to the floor. All our non-Christian friends snapped up in their seats with a simultaneous jerk, and Coleman pronounced us man and wife. What a kiss! What bliss! We ran up the aisle, I threw my arms around Kai, and laughed, "We did it. We did it!" I never thought it would happen to me. I was a married woman, "finally."

The Honeymoon

We were nervous. Two veterans of romance stood and faced each other in the Westgate Hotel bridal suite, unsure of how to proceed. A colorful tower of boxes and ribbons were gaily heaped into one corner of the room, and flowers glorified every corner, mantel, and shelf. And the bed stretched self-indulgently across the room like a corpulent throne.

Gingerly, Kai took the blond 7-11 hairpins out of my hair, one by one, and removed my veil, laying it lovingly on a lounge chair. He took my face in his hands and kissed me. His hands were shaking and my knees were watery. Self-consciously he examined the buttons on my gown, delicately unfastening each one, cautiously trying to avoid damage to my Cinderella dress. I loosened his tie and peeled off his jacket. The tension was exhausting. He kissed me again, I fell into him, and we both fell on the bed.

"You'd think a man of the world, with two marriages and eight children, would be an old hand at this," he said, "but I feel as though this is the first time for me."

"Me too," was all I could whisper.

The next morning we flew to a cabin in Vermont. The leaves were burning in the full blaze of autumn, and the mirrored surface of a nearby pond captured the still-life pictures of summer turned ancient.

A dozen red and yellow roses were waiting in the cabin with a note that said, "To my beloved wife, Danuta. Welcome to our honeymoon. I love you. Your husband, Kai."

When Kai had told me earlier of this cabin near the Sugar Bush ski resort, he was rather unexplicit. "It's beautiful," he said.

"Well, what do you mean by *beautiful*?" I asked, expecting details.

"I'm not exactly sure of the precise details," Kai apologized, "but the friend who recommended it said it would be perfect for us."

"Does it have a fireplace?" I asked eagerly, trying to fill in the blanks.

"I'm sure it does." Kai did not sound sure at all.

"But did you ask?" I said.

"No, but a cabin in Vermont is certain to have one," Kai cheerfully added.

"Darling, would you please call and find out?"

Kai came back from the phone call looking pleased. "Well, I called, and it does have a fireplace!"

"What kind of furniture does it have?" I asked.

"Oh, well, I didn't ask about the furniture."

"All right, but did you ask about the color of the carpet?"

"The color of the carpet?"

"Kai, how do you know what kind of a place we're going to spend our entire honeymoon in unless you ask about the carpet?"

"What does the color of the carpet have to do with what kind of a place it is?"

"Well, suppose they say it has an orange shag carpet," I tried to explain. "Does that give you an idea of what kind of a place to expect? You can already picture bare spots in it, and what kind of furniture goes with bare spots and orange shag? Garage sale furniture, that's what! Who wants to spend a honeymoon at a garage sale? Now, if they say 'rice paper white carpet,' you sort of get a picture of luxury, right? I mean, after all, nobody would put a rusty bedspring and a lumpy mattress on a white carpet, would they?"

Kai listened with a look of amazement on his face. He gave me the phone number. I learned the carpet was high-quality, silver-gray, indoor-outdoor carpet, and the furniture was modern Scandinavian. The cabin had a fully equipped kitchen, three bedrooms, one pull-out bed next to the fireplace, and an ample supply of firewood on the doorstep. I knew it would be perfect, just as Kai said it would be.

For the first three days we stayed indoors, eating homemade lentil soup and chocolates. By the fourth day lentil soup was losing its appeal, so we explored the small town of Warren, bought some cuddly sweaters in a woolens store, and climbed Sugar Bush Mountain. I took three dozen pictures of the most stunning autumn scenes I have ever seen, all with the lens cap on.

Our honeymoon was not all fun and games. Kai was trying to negotiate a mortgage loan on a home I had found in Chesapeake, Virginia. I had called a real estate agent and asked what she had in the way of a house with a fireplace, a barn, and a corral, on a big piece of land, secluded from the road, surrounded by trees.

Quite by accident, the listing book literally fell open to the pictures of the very home I had just described.

"I'll come by and pick you up," she said, "and I'll have a whole list of homes we can look at."

The first house we saw was the one that fell out of the listing book. It was the quintessential "house in the country" that I had always dreamed of living in one day. I pictured rose gardens, vegetable gardens, long walks in the woods in the fall, trampling crispy golden leaves underfoot. I didn't look at any other house. This was our house. Now all I had to do was to tell Kai.

"Kai! Darling, I've found the house we're going to buy!" I gushed over the phone.

"Are we going to buy a house?" I had caught him off guard.

"I know we didn't talk about this when you left, but I think I've found the perfect place for us, Kai. You must see it, quickly, before somebody else buys it!"

Kai flew back out from California the next day to see "our house." The first thing he said as he rounded the driveway and looked at three and a half acres of grounds was, "Who's going to cut the grass?"

I ignored the question and tried to point out the wonderfulness of the house. Kai kept on eyeing the lawn. I was devastated. He didn't share my vision for this house. He didn't see my rose garden, or the artist's loft with skylights I imagined in the barn, or the perfect place to put the Christmas tree. But gradually it grew on him, and before long Kai was trying desperately to get a bank in Virginia to loan us the money to buy the house.

The problem was that nobody in Virginia had ever heard of Kai Soderman, and the banks were not parting with their money for a man who had no residency in the state yet, held no "regular nine-to-five job" since he was very successfully self-employed, and who had no business associates in Virginia with whom he could establish a professional working relationship, or who would vouch for him. Banks would not accept my account since I was married now. They preferred to do it the old-fashioned way and base their loan on the value of the husband, rather than the wife. It was a frantic time for Kai. Nobody was listening to him and nobody came to help.

What made matters even worse was that Kai was trying to negotiate all of this over the phone, from Vermont, on his honeymoon. He would make five or six calls a day, and he was getting more and more disheartened.

On the fourth day of our honeymoon, Kai gave me a mischievous look and said, "How would you like to meet my mother?"

"Your mother? I'd love to meet your mother! I love your mother! But your mother lives in Sweden!"

"So, how would you like to meet her?"

I squealed with delight. We packed our things into the rental car with JUST MARRIED painted on the back window, and drove to Montreal to catch a Finnair jumbo jet to Stockholm, Sweden.

We were going to fly business class to Stockholm but we ended up with too much luggage, including Kai's guitar, my wedding bouquet, and the semialive red and yellow roses I took with me from Vermont. We also had my entire wedding trousseau and all of Kai's immediate-needs luggage, since he was going straight from the honeymoon to Virginia, with no extra trips back to California to pack. In all, we had ten pieces of luggage, and nowhere to store the carryon bags with any comfort in the surprisingly cramped quarters of business class. Kai went forward to speak with the chief flight attendant, who agreed to let us transfer to first class and pay the difference on the ticket in Stockholm.

Halfway across the Atlantic, the flight attendants noticed us clinging and cooing to each other, and with a sparkle in her eyes, the chief attendant called Kai into the galley.

"We have noticed the two of you so much in love," said the attendant, "and we have been talking with one another. We decided that you two have been so pleasant and wonderful to serve that we would like to give you a wedding gift. We are not going to charge you for your first-class tickets."

The Lord was blessing us, and we were literally flying high.

I loved Stockholm. I loved the snow and the waterways winding through the city, below magnificent buildings. The Venice of the North enchanted me. But most thrilling was meeting Kai's beautiful mother.

She greeted us at the door of her apartment with hugs and kisses, as though she had known me all my life. Kai had spoken of me for so many years that Agnes had long ago come to love me. Perhaps it was her prayers that initiated our marriage after all. Agnes Soderman is small in stature but regal in nature. I loved her immediately, and although I didn't speak Swedish and she didn't speak English very well at the time, we got along famously, chatting about all sorts of things like long-lost friends.

During our week in Stockholm I met Bo, Kai's brother, and his wife, Inger, and we listened to a group of jazz musicians who came by his home and jammed into the wee hours of the night. Bo Soderman, though a very successful businessman in his own right, is also a terrific jazz and classical pianist. It was a treat to hear Kai's resonant voice singing ballads and gospel tunes with Bo's jazz accompaniment.

Kai was the rage of Sweden in his late teens and early twenties. He was known as a singing sensation and his records were compared to those of Frank Sinatra. Long before Kai became a businessman, he was a balladeer, and even today people are always asking him to sing. Our first day in Stockholm, we hailed a taxi to the hotel, and the cabdriver kept looking in the rearview mirror at us. I thought he was looking at me, since I've become used to being recognized, although I couldn't understand how a driver in Sweden would recognize me, since the "700 Club" doesn't reach Stockholm yet.

Finally, the driver turned back to us and said, "Hey, aren't you Kai Soderman, the singer?"

"Wow!" I said, "you really are famous here!" It was thirty years since Kai had a singing career in Sweden.

But after a week, the cold was getting to me. I needed sunshine and warmth. We both did. So we flew to Portugal, to the southern coast called the Algarve.

It was here, in a villa overlooking the Straits of Gibraltar, that we discovered "our song." The full-bodied orange moon was rising over the sea from Tangier. It was midnight, and we were sitting on the veranda listening to the wind rustling the bougainvilleas that were hanging overhead. The sea below sparkled with moon dust. I saw Kai's half-face in the moonlight, looking at me. He picked up his guitar and began to sing.

I can never let a full moon go by now without hearing Kai sing "Blue Moon" to me. And I can never see a full moon without remembering how it looks rising over the African continent, with the wind and the bougainvilleas and the veranda in Villa Lara. I'm a sucker for romance.

But something else happened that night in Algarve that will forever remain etched in my brain. I was getting ready for bed, filled with love and the fire of the moon and the night. I tucked myself in between the sheets and waited for Kai. After about ten minutes, I began to worry that something had happened to him, so I called for him. At that moment, appearing from out of the shadows on the veranda, and stepping through the open brick archway that served as a window, stood a man I had never seen before. His moustache was penciled over his upper lip, and he was wearing only his guitar, a bandanna around his neck, and goose bumps.

"Good evening," he purred. "I heard you were here in the villa, and I came as quickly as I could."

"Who are you?" I giggled, going along with the game.

"Why, don't you know who I am?"

"Well, no, not exactly. . ." I said, holding the sheet up to my nose in an act of modesty.

"Well, my dear, I am the Treat of Villa Lara! I am the welcoming committee for every beautiful lady who visits the Algarve!"

"The Treat of Villa Lara! Oh, I've heard of you! I'm so pleased to make your acquaintance, sir."

"Well, of course you have heard of me," he said, strutting about the room with his stomach sucked in and his chest pushed out. "I'm world famous! Would you care to tango?" With that, he threw both arms out, the guitar strap broke, and the guitar fell down. Now he was only wearing a bandanna and goose bumps. I laughed so hard my face hurt.

Even today, "the Treat" makes an occasional personal appearance just to say hello.

The day we left Villa Lara, I cried. "I don't want our honeymoon to end, Kai!"

Kai put his arms around me. "Don't worry, my darling. I promise you that our honeymoon will never end."

We packed up our ten bags and took a flight from a nearby Portuguese village called Faro to the capital city of Lisbon, where we were going to catch a TWA flight to New York.

During the past few days, there had been torrential rainstorms in Portugal, the first good rain in that country in nearly three years, we were told. For that reason, dozens of airline flights to and from Lisbon had been delayed or canceled altogether. The airport was a zoo, packed with thousands of angry, confused, and disgruntled passengers from all around the world. It seemed as if no two people spoke the same language, and tempers were short.

We were poured into the terminal with the thousands of others who had no clue where customs was, where the international terminal was, where to get your bags checked in, or even where to get a boarding pass. There were no signs in the airport. We were pushing two shopping carts piled high with ten pieces of luggage, up and down the terminal, through the crowds, the smoke, and the smells, looking for information.

Someone told us that we needed *los stampos* pasted to the back of our tickets before we could get out of the airport. This was an airport tax every passenger was obliged to pay in Lisbon. We stood in a long line for almost an hour to purchase the stamps, but when we finally reached the window, the clerk refused to take Portuguese currency and directed us to *el banco,* where we were instructed to get American dollars to buy *los stampos*. There was another line at the bank.

With American currency in hand, we filed back to the hour-long line, still dragging our ten bags and two shopping carts with us, and purchased the stamps for our tickets.

The next task was to get boarding passes. We found the TWA counter, handed over the ten bags, acquired the boarding passes, and then were told the plane was already leaving. A TWA clerk took charge and led us down into the bowels of the airport, where more than two thousand people were mobbing the customs desk, crushing and pushing and growling. The clerk forged into this human jam, clearing a path, shouting at the top of her lungs, ''Make clear, make clear, these are Americans! They are late for their plane! First-class passengers coming through! Make clear, make clear!''

She was already far into the crowd ahead of us, and we were

unable to ask her to cool it on the "Make clear, these are Americans" speech. The deeper we plunged into the mob, the more hostile it became.

As we worked our way through to the front, a man in the crowd snarled, "Who do you think you are, coming to the head of the line? You people should stand back here for hours like the rest of us!" With that, the man shoved me with his elbow and I lost Kai's hand. Two more men shouldered themselves between us. Kai broke past them, reached for my hand, and pulled me toward him. I was carrying my red and yellow roses from Vermont, my wedding bouquet, and the bunch of flowers I found waiting for us in the hotel in Stockholm. They were all getting crushed and the lace bow that tied them together was coming undone. So was Kai.

The first man to shove me now shoved Kai off balance. By this time I was up to the customs counter, when I heard a very angry Swedish voice growling through clenched teeth, "You shove one more time, buddy, and you're going to find yourself shoved all the way into the next building!"

The other guy yelled back, "Oh, yeah?" and started coming after Kai through the crowd. The customs man leaped across the counter, hollering something in Portuguese.

"Kai!" was all I said. I had never seen my mild-mannered Swedish balladeer angry before, much less ready to come to blows with a couple thousand people.

Kai walked over to me and said, "I'm sorry, Danuta. I guess I wasn't much of a Christian witness, was I? I haven't been in a fight since high school!" A few seconds later, seeing that I was still a little nervous, he said, "I couldn't have hit the guy anyway—I have my hands full!" And he lifted up both arms, clutching four large carryon bags and his guitar case. We both managed to smile.

Kai was really feeling bad about losing his temper. "I'm going to go back there and apologize to that guy. There's no reason for any of us to get angry with one another. After all, we are all victims of this turmoil, and no one is to blame."

I talked him out of returning to that throng, but my admiration for him grew enormously. The man has a good, strong heart.

The helpful clerk who nearly got us killed had disappeared, so now all we had to do was find our plane. With no signs designating flight numbers or airline carriers, passengers bound for New York huddled together and wandered up and down the two flights of stairs, changing directions like a school of fish, following rumors of where TWA might have parked a bird.

Finally, we walked out into the cool, fresh air, away from the stifling pandemonium behind us, toward that big, gorgeous American airplane. As we boarded, a blond flight attendant with two ponytails snapped her bubble gum and said, "Hi, y'all." Ah, the sweet, unmistakable voice of an American!

As we sat down in the air-conditioned comfort of the jet, the captain's Texas drawl came over the intercom: "Howdy, ladies and gentlemen. Welcome to TWA, bound for JFK, in the good ol' U S of A." As far as we were concerned, we were already home.

But little did we know what "home" was going to be.

Chapter Nine
The Wild Kingdom

My wedding trousseau was lost somewhere between New York and Virginia Beach. We traveled halfway around the world for a month, lugging ten pieces of luggage, to lose two pieces on the last leg home. I was upset, not just because I lost two pieces of luggage but because they were the most precious pieces.

In those two bags were pictures of Vermont, when the lens cap was off, two sweaters Kai bought for me in that little woolens shop, my honeymoon nightgown, my white slippers, and my new white satin robe. There was hosiery with autumn leaves painted on the stockings, pictures from the day we announced our engagement, photographs of the only bridal shower I ever went to—my own—one full ounce of my favorite perfume, a locket my brothers gave me to wear as something old with my gown, and from my mother, two small diamond earrings and a delicate platinum bracelet. They were the only valuable pieces of jewelry my mother owned, and she gave them to me for my wedding day . . . now they were gone.

I tried to tell myself they were just things, and things are not important, but these were special mementos given to me by my family, and somebody stole it all, right off the carousel going to the plane. It took me a whole year to tell my mother I had lost those little shiny stones.

When I was growing up, we didn't have anything to lose or to steal. My father was a Polish war hero and a sculptor, an artist who worked in wood and stone for churches all over the country. So we moved constantly and never had much money. Once we even lived in a tent, in an attic another time, and picked cherries and beans and dug up potatoes with our hands from a snow-laden field, gleaning after the tractors had harvested the crop.

Things were not important then, and things were not to be important to me now, either. The Lord had given me a lesson: Nobody can steal your memories. Look to tomorrow, remember yesterday, but cling to nothing but Him, and to my dearest husband, Kai. That was what was important. But I still hope for the day when those two miserable little bags will be standing on our doorstep with a note that says, "Sorry, we accidentally stole your bags and our guilty conscience won't let us keep them any longer."

We still could not buy the home we loved. That beautiful house sat like a jewel in the country, shimmering, beckoning, untouchable. Kai struggled to acquire the loan for the house. He met with every bank executive in the city, and they all gave him the same old runaround: "Well, I'm sorry Mr. Soderman, you just haven't lived in Virginia long enough, and we will only accept your residency status, not your wife's." Or, "Fill out another loan application and show your income tax records from the last three years, and oh, yes, by the way, what was that bankruptcy about ten years ago?''

Kai explained about his divorce, moving to Sweden, filing for bankruptcy but paying everybody off, and having no creditors from that time . . . but still, nobody was listening.

Kai had moved his office to Virginia Beach and was working as a financial consultant and investment broker, but it took time to build up a new clientele on the East Coast, and he had just scraped his life together a few years before. How could he explain to bankers the despair of the past, and the momentum of the future? There were days when, coming home from work, I found Kai sitting in our rental house, deeply discouraged, pounded down by rejection, but with plenty of fight in him to try again tomorrow to get our home.

When I asked him why he worked so hard to get that house, he told me, ''Because you love it so much, and now I do, too. I want to make you happy. Besides, it's a challenge to accomplish a difficult task.'' But it was a challenge that took its toll on us. We weren't laughing very much anymore.

And then one day in prayer, we asked the Lord for extra guidance, for a sign that what we were trying to accomplish was what He wanted for us. We were beginning to doubt that we should have that house. And the Bible fell open to Joshua, chapter 1:

> Now therefore arise, go over this Jordan, thou, and all this people, unto the land which I do give to them, even to the children of Israel. Every place that the sole of your foot shall tread upon, that have I given unto you. . . . Be strong and of a good courage: for unto this people shalt thou divide for an inheritance the land. . . . Be strong and of good

courage; be not afraid, neither be thou dismayed: for the
Lord thy God is with thee whithersoever thou goest.

Joshua 1:2–9

The day after we read that Scripture, Kai stopped trying to take
control of the situation. In fact, when he met with the last banker
that day, he didn't try very hard to convince him of the efficacy
of loaning us the money. Kai didn't push any papers in front of
the man, and he offered no defensive arguments. And the banker
beamed at Kai, "Well, Mr. Soderman, that sounds good to us.
You've got yourself a house!"

It was a good thing we got that house, too, because my mother
was driving cross-country, with her two dogs, two lovebirds, and
four cats, to move into a house that we didn't even have until two
days before she arrived. It's called *faith*.

We took possession of our home December 17, 1983, exactly
six years from the day we met. We had invited my mother to live
with us in the wide-open spaces of the Virginia countryside.

My father was a dashing Polish soldier when he met my English mother in London, just after the war. I was born in England,
but we emigrated to Canada, and later the United States, when I
was three years old.

My parents were divorced when I was seventeen. My father
died during my sophomore year in college, and my mother raised
two boys, Michael and Paul, on her own. She had a rough time
of it, working as a nurse, sometimes pulling double shifts, usually as a floor supervisor in a local hospital, and mothering two
small boys. Her life left little time for leisure or sleep. She
sacrificed for us all her life. Now it was my turn to give back to
her a little of what she had given us.

With the youngest member of the family turning eighteen, and
ready to go off to school on his own soon, Mom would be living

alone in San Diego. We thought it would be wonderful for her to move in with us, where there was plenty of space and room for her to garden. Perhaps for the first time in her life, she could enjoy living, rather than struggling for existence.

Among the menagerie my mom tended and loved in San Diego was a sheep named Emma and two ducks—not bad for living in a condominium with a postage-stamp garden. Kai felt that in order to make Mom feel at home "on the range," he should get Emma transported from California to Virginia. What better way to transport a sheep than by flying the friendly skies! He called United Airlines and had Emma flown out in the largest carrier made.

It was a blustery November day when we pulled in to the freight office to pick up our pet sheep. A harried-looking man packed in sweaters and oily dungarees came toward us in the cavernous warehouse, wiping his hands on an oily rag. He seemed distracted, as if he were missing his lunch break, and he barely looked up at us when he asked us for the claim number for our precious cargo. We followed him past several crates and boxes sitting on the floor, and after inspecting the top of the carrier for the claim number, he said, "Here."

I ran to the front of the carrier, eager to see how Emma made out on her transcontinental flight. I began calling her name: "Oh, Emma! Hello, Emma! Pretty Emma!"

Emma poked her black nose up to the wire grid and twitched her ears. Tufts of grubby, woolly curls sprouted out of her forehead, and she was licking her little chin, recognizing her name.

Somewhat curious, the warehouse man tipped his head to the side and all too briefly peeked into the carrier. He quickly stood erect and looked at us for the first time, and with his eyes bulging wide, slowly looked back into the carrier again as he said in a slow, southern drawl, "Lady, that is the ugliest dawg I have ever seen!"

The warehouse man clucked and shook his head as he helped shove the carrier into a borrowed van. We watched him in the rearview mirror, scratching his head as we drove away. We didn't have the heart to tell him Emma was a sheep.

We brought her back to the rental house, where I had cornered off a quadrant of the garage with large bales of hay and several spare tires. Emma now had a first-class home in the suburbs.

The next morning, Kai had an early business meeting to attend and quietly dressed, leaving me snoozing for another half hour. He went to the garage to get into his car and stopped to give Emma a pat on the head. He had never actually seen a sheep up close. Kai was a Swedish city boy, having moved to Stockholm from Lapland. He didn't have the intuitive sense of a farmer, but he put himself in Emma's place for a minute, imagining what it must have been like for a sheep to be cooped up in a dog kennel on a coast-to-coast flight, and he sympathized.

Kai figured Emma wanted to stretch her legs, and probably needed to find a fire hydrant. My mom had sent us her basset hound the day before, and since the dog needed walking, Kai assumed the sheep did, too. He put a leash on the basset hound and made a makeshift leash out of an electrical extension cord for Emma. It was a sight to see. A tall, elegant, businessman, in a suit and tie, walking down a suburban street with a basset hound on one leash and a sheep the size of a small couch on the other!

The day we actually moved into our house was a glorious day! The sun battered the last leaves of autumn and the day was cold and bright and milky golden. We ceremoniously encouraged Emma into the corral, and all three of us—Mom, Kai, and I— stared at her and sighed deep sighs, contentedly. Emma was home. That meant we were home. And that meant that Hushy the basset hound, Dobie the Doberman, Sweets, a Doberman I had befriended, Nietzsche, my calico cat, Noots, Kai's calico cat, Kiki, the Siamese, Boots, a stray cat we found and raised, Mr. Nimo, a twenty-five-pound white Angora cat I rescued from the pound, Niki, another beautiful stray, a foster golden retriever we were temporarily keeping for my brother, two ducks, and two turtledoves, unnamed, all lived on what became known as The Wild Kingdom. Not a bad country start for two people used to living in condominiums on the beach in California!

Pat and Ben insisted we call our place Green Acres, since a blond television host and a businessman living on a sort-of-farm fit the model of that old comedy series. Kai and I found ourselves referring to the homestead as The Wild Kingdom, and for good reason!

We live only a few miles from the Great Dismal Swamp (no joke!), and that means we live with bugs and animals that even Adam didn't get around to naming!

One morning I gazed out of the upstairs window to see what I thought at first to be a large paper bag blowing across the driveway. The problem was, paper bags don't have four feet. It was a snapping turtle the size of a toilet-seat lid, and it was slowly making its way to our ducks! Streaking across my brain were mental pictures of snapping turtles whacking off limbs with a mighty chomp, and didn't someone once tell me that if a snapping turtle clamps down on, say, your arm, his jaws lock so tightly that you have to race to the hospital to sever its head and release your arm? That did it. I screamed for our gardener, Jaye. He cracked off a thick branch from a nearby tree and presented it to the reptile. The turtle responded with vigor and tightened down on that small piece of timber so fiercely that Jaye was able to pick up the branch, turtle dangling, and scurry him back to the swamp where he belonged.

Kai really got into the swing of living on The Wild Kingdom. One morning, looking up from my coffee cup, I caught a glimpse of him in the hall. He had on his new cowboy boots, his new cowboy hat, his new cowboy belt and buckle, his new "ranch hand" jacket, and his new leather gloves.

"Where are you going, honey?" I asked.

Kai stood in the doorway, growing taller by the second. He spread his feet wide, cocked his head, and squinted his eyes. He pounded his fisted, gloved hand into the palm of the other hand, took a deep breath, and in a slow, southern, country, Swedish, John Wayne drawl, he said, "I'm gonna feed Emma." He walked the 150 yards toward the barn with the confident swagger of a man who had come into his own.

Our two ducks, Gustav and Sophia, are named for the king and queen of Sweden. My mother bought the yellow, fluffy ducklings in a feed store one day for Paul, the youngest family member. The ducks learned to swim in the bathtub when they were little, but now they were ten pounds each of feet and feathers. Mom left them on a farm in San Diego County before coming to Virginia Beach. After all, she had the turtledoves, the three cats, and two dogs with her, as well as a few things of her own in that car. There was no room for two ducks, but she missed them. It so happened that Kai had a business meeting in San Diego and to surprise my mother, he planned to return with the ducks. It was easier said than done.

Kai picked them up in a small kennel the day before he left California. Then he drove into the city to find overnight accommodations at the luxurious New Intercontinental Hotel. There he stood at the check-in counter in the plush hotel lobby, carrying his briefcase in one hand and two ducks in a cage in the other.

"Yes sir, can I help you?" the man behind the counter asked, with his eyes drifting over to Gustav and Sophia.

"You have a suite for Soderman?" Kai inquired.

"Uh, yes sir," the young man replied, "but sir, aren't those ducks you have there?"

"Yes, as a matter of fact they are," Kai chuckled, "but don't worry, they're with me."

"Well, uh, sir, we don't, uh, take ducks."

"Could you possibly keep them in the gym overnight?"

"Uh, no sir, we really couldn't do that. . . ."

"How about the basement?"

There was no room at the inn for ducks. Kai drove them back to the farm. The next morning he learned that the airlines wouldn't take the ducks unless they had a certificate of health. He called a local vet and had him dash out to check the birds over. Mary Phillips, the pastor's wife of our church in California, saved the day. She brought the ducks to the airport just as Kai was checking in, complete with the document of health needed by the airlines.

"Uh, sir, aren't those ducks you have with you?" The flight attendant asked.

"Yes, yes, they are." Kai knew what was coming next.

"Well, uh, sir, I don't think we can keep them up here in first class. . . ."

The ducks flew back to Virginia Beach in the storage compartment of the plane, along with the baggage. But Kai was so concerned for their health that he had the flight attendant check on them at a stopover in Atlanta. They arrived—all three of them—safe and sound. Mom was happy. And that made it all worthwhile.

Of all the creatures we had to learn to live with—mosquitoes the size of hummingbirds, furry bugs too big to fit into mason jars, Japanese beetles, voracious fleas, kamikaze horseflies, monster hairy spiders, carpenter bees as large as your thumb that drill into the lumber of your house, miniature luminescent green frogs

that cling to the doorjamb with suction-cup feet to slurp up un-
suspecting bugs that buzz toward the porch light—the creatures
we really find most offensive are snakes.

Living within a few miles of the Great Dismal Swamp makes
one susceptible to the great dismal creatures of the swamp. One
of the first horror stories we heard upon moving to the area was
that fishermen along the brackish canals of the waterways often
have snakes actually fall into their boats from overhead trees. If
that had ever happened to Kai and me, we would have immediately recognized the new proprietor of the boat, and simulta-
neously and voluntarily dived into the water. The big problem is,
of course, that's where snakes live, too! It was not easy for a
California condo couple to get used to the country kingdom. So
we decided to educate ourselves about our fellow beasts, and take
a snake course at the local swamp refuge park.

It was there we learned that out of the dozens of indigenous
snakes, only three are poisonous, and possibly fatal: rattlesnakes,
copperheads, and cottonmouths.

We learned of various ways to tell whether or not a snake is
poisonous. One way is by observing the scales underneath the
snake's belly, as they grow toward the tail, past the anus. I didn't
actually catch how you could tell by observing those scales, since
I was absolutely certain I would never get close enough to a
snake's anus to investigate. Another way to tell is to notice the
shape of the pupil of a snake's eye. A diamond-shaped pupil
spells trouble. But who's going to look a snake square in the face
to find out if it will kill you? We learned a little rhyme that
helped:

                    Red and black,
                    Look out Jack!

Red and yellow,
Kill a fellow!

That means if the colors red and black are adjoining on a snake, chances are the critter isn't harmful, but if red and yellow are back to back, you have a poisonous snake. Another method of determining whether or not a snake is poisonous is in the way it slithers. Generally speaking, we learned, a snake is poisonous if it slithers with its head raised. A nonpoisonous snake merely trucks along with his nose to the ground. We handled a couple of snakes in the seminar, to get familiar with snakes that don't bite, like the blacksnake, "the farmer's friend." Blacksnakes eat mice and rats and eggs, and are generally tolerated because they earn their keep.

We walked away from the seminar feeling somewhat equipped to handle whatever snake emergency we might be confronted with, comfortable in our knowledge that snakes are, after all, just snakes. We soon found our composure tested.

Early one summery Saturday morning, I was exercising with a workout tape in the living room when Kai yelled for me from the study. He was staring out the window at what could be identified at once as a poisonous snake: its head was lifted off the ground as it wound its way across the lawn. It was a dull orange, and I was sure that if I looked that viper in the eye, it would have diamond-shaped pupils.

"It's a copperhead," Kai announced. I agreed. "Well, let's go get him!" Kai sounded strong.

I dashed out the door to keep an eye on the snake, while Kai went for tools. More than a few minutes had passed when Kai appeared with the utensils of destruction, a hoe and a shovel.

The snake started to move again. It was a peculiar parade. I was right behind the copperhead in my bare feet and leotards, with the hoe high above my head, ready to hack at a moment's notice. Kai was behind me, having changed from his shorts and tennis shoes to his blue jeans, boots, and long-sleeved shirt, with the shovel raised above his head, ready to whack at the snake if, for some reason, I should miss.

The three of us—the snake, Kai, and I—filed across the lawn as though in some primitive dance, two of us with arms raised above our heads, tools waving in the air, stalking with bent knee. Then suddenly the snake stopped. It took me two steps to notice. I was nearly upon it. I screamed. The snake slowly turned his head around 180 degrees and stared at me. I froze with my hoe high. The snake waited. I lifted the hoe even higher. Nobody breathed. I lifted the hoe just a big higher. The snake was motionless, watching and waiting.

Eternity filled the moment as time stood still. The air was stifling. Ancient reptilian eyes, filled with contempt, were riveted to mine. I felt not fear but revulsion, yes, a dreaded fascination that revived some dark and primal past between us.

"Go on, get him! Get him!" Kai whispered.

From the corner of my eye, I saw Kai at least twenty steps behind me!

"I can't!" I yelled back. "Not while he's watching me!" I took a giant step backward. "I just can't kill it!" I moaned. "Kai, what are you doing back there? You kill it! You've got the boots and the jeans and the long-sleeved shirt!"

Kai put down the shovel. "I can't kill it, either."

So he jumped into the Cadillac and drove across the road to our neighbor's house. Billy was born in these parts. He knew about these things. He understood country. Billy drove up in his truck. He was in his shorts, barefoot.

"Yep, that's a copperhead, all right," he said. "Just look at the size of him, too. He's a big 'un."

And with that, he took Kai's shovel and plunked it into the ground with one hand, killing the Dismal Swamp creature.

The next day Kai came home with a gun. I hate guns. I didn't want one in the house. I didn't want it in the barn. I didn't want it on the property. Kai explained that this was no ordinary gun. It was a snake gun. It didn't just shoot a bullet—it sprayed lots of little pellets. Well, a snake gun. That was different. I could tolerate a snake gun. Just as long as it wasn't a real gun.

I forgot about the snake gun for a long time, until one day when I was in the barn with the ducks. One of the females (we now had four) was brooding and she had four beautiful eggs in her nest. From under the mama's breast popped a fluffy little yellow head, peep, peeping for all the world to hear. We had a baby!

Kai suggested we take the chick in the house since a dark old barn is susceptible to rats who eat chicks at night. We fashioned a cardboard box, laid down warm toweling, and kept it in the sun in the bathroom. This duckling was the most perfect little thing we had ever seen. A perfectly round head, a perfectly formed little yellow beak, perfectly huge yellow feet. We named it "Perfect" and hand-fed it daily until it was strong enough to take care of itself with the others.

The next morning I dashed out to the barn, expecting to see three more yellow heads bobbing up from the nest. I nudged the mama off her nest and found only one egg! Eagerly I looked for the two missing chicks, thinking they had hatched, but there was no sign of eggshells, no sign of chicks. I looked in the second stall and noticed a large bale of hay had fallen from the shelf. I bent down to pick the bale up and saw, in the corner, in the dark, a piece of old rubber tire. *Funny,* I thought, *I didn't think we had any old rubber tires in here.* I bent down to look again, and what I saw horrified me.

There, entwined in the corner of the stall, was a huge black-snake. It took my breath away. I gulped down some air and remembered that "a blacksnake is the farmer's friend. It only eats rats, mice, and eggs." *Eggs!* My duck eggs!

"Jaye!" I hollered for the gardener. "Jaye! Hurry!"

Jaye plunged into the stall with the hoe. I was behind him, pushing him forward. "Jaye, get that filthy thing. Get him, Jaye, get him!" I didn't know that Jaye had dropped his glasses and couldn't see what he was doing. He blindly hacked away at the snake anyhow, and killed it. He picked it up with a stick and brought it out in the open to show Kai, who had come running. And that's when I noticed two huge bumps in the snake's long, limp body.

"My eggs!" I angrily pointed. "That snake ate my eggs!" I suddenly became quiet. "Snakes swallow things whole, don't they?"

"Yeah?" Jaye and Kai chorused.

"And those eggs are up in the front of the snake, which means he hasn't had them too long. . . ." I trailed off in my own thoughts.

Kai looked at Jaye. "Are you ready for what she's going to say next, Jaye?"

I finished my sentence as though it were uninterrupted. ". . . I bet if we split this thing open, we could rescue those little eggs!" I flashed my expectant eyes first at Kai and then at Jaye. They were recoiling from the very idea.

"I warned you," Kai said to Jaye.

"Well, I don't know, Danuta," Jaye said, scratching his head and screwing up his face.

"I'll get the knife," I volunteered, bounding into the house and back, with an old bread knife.

"So who's going in there after my eggs?" I asked.

"Let's draw straws," Jaye said.

"All right," Kai said, "but even if I lose, I can't do it."

"Me neither," I chickened out. "Besides, Jaye, you're the gardener!"

With a deep breath, Jaye bent down and started to cut away at the snake with his eyes closed, slicing between the front and the back of the first bump. An egg slid out, bleeding yellow. It was broken.

"Try the other one," I prodded.

The same procedure produced a perfect egg. It slid out from the snake's belly as though in birth. My egg was born again!

I tenderly cradled it in the palm of my hand and wiped the visceral slime from the shell. How close this little egg had come to death and destruction in the belly of the viper! I marveled at the precious gem in my hand, and saw tiny wet feathers pressing against the inside of its calcium crust.

All of mankind is like that one little egg, snatched from certain death by a Savior. Just as this tiny life was born again, so were we all, when Christ crushed the head of Satan and split open the bowels of hell. In Him we are born again, given another chance to live. And so, as this insignificant life was spared, I was in the hand of God, cradled in His love, my sins wiped away. I ran the egg back to the nest and tucked it underneath the mama duck.

"If this little duck lives, I'm going to name it Jonah!" I vowed. "If God could rescue Jonah from the belly of a whale, He can save this Jonah from the belly of a snake!"

The next day, Jonah was still in the nest. That was a good sign. I had noticed that the brooding duck would destroy eggs she didn't want, but she was tenderly nurturing this one. But I was not prepared to see another blacksnake arrogantly curled up against the nest, waiting to test its jaws against that which was already saved! Now I was mad. I screamed for Kai and went for the hoe. I managed to pin him down, hoping Kai would come quickly and finish him off. Kai burst in with the snake gun.

"Step back!" he shouted as he aimed the barrel at the snake's head.

"Wait a minute, Kai! I've already got it pinned down!"

"Step back! I'll get it with the gun!"

I let go of the hoe and the snake wriggled free and made for the corner. Kai blasted at it with the snake gun. *Ka-boom!* Shells ricocheted off the cement wall, hay splattered everywhere. But the snake kept going. Kai fired again. *Ka-boom! Splat!* The shells smeared against the wall and the earthen hay-covered floor. But the snake kept going. Going. Gone. It disappeared between the wall and the floor of the stall. Kai loaded the snake gun and pointed the barrel right into the snake hole. *Ka-boom!* Mud blasted back into our faces, smearing the wall, caking our clothes. A huge hole was left in the ground. And the snake was gone.

"You missed?" I cried, drenched in mud, heart racing.

Perspiration poured down Kai's face. He went back to look at the hole. He couldn't believe it, either.

I picked up a shovel and began to dig into the dirt. It had rained hard the night before and the water table was only a foot below. "Snakes can't hold their breath that long underwater," I said, with a new surge of energy. Suddenly there it was, coiled into a ball in the mud.

Kai threw down the snake gun and grabbed the hoe. The snake began to lunge at him. Kai answered with a series of tremendous blows of the hoe, screaming at the black nemesis, "I'm going to get you!" Then he shouted something in Swedish I didn't understand. The first blows hit the wall and the mud puddle, but eventually the hoe hit its target. Kai delivered a dozen blows to the snake, just to make sure it was dead. It was very dead. He turned to me, exhausted, panting, perspiring, and I ran into his arms.

"Oh, Kai! You killed it! You saved the eggs!"

From that day on, Kai has never shirked snake duty. Jonah didn't make it. One of the papa ducks accidentally stepped on the egg before it hatched. But we'll name the next one Jonah in memory of that summer, and the tenaciousness of life on The Wild Kingdom.

There is another kind of adventure on The Wild Kingdom, just as intense but far more sublime. . . . Romance!

Chapter Ten
Staying in Love

e celebrate our wedding anniversaries monthly. We do this for several reasons. First, to keep count. As a former Anti-Bride, I can't believe that I have a relationship with just one man that has lasted longer than a few months. This accumulation of months encourages and astonishes me. It makes me feel as though we are making up for all the time we spent apart when we should have been together! Second, it's fun. We have something to look forward to each month, a time when we can renew our pledge to each other, refresh our love, and stir up the embers of passion. And third, it gives us a chance to stretch our imaginations in ways of expressing our love to each other.

For our eleven-month anniversary, Kai arranged for the rental of a couple of Arabian horses which were to be brought to the house for two hours of riding lessons. It was a wonderful idea, except things didn't work out exactly the way he planned.

The woman with whom he negotiated the rental had only one trailer and needed to borrow her next-door neighbor's trailer for the second horse. Then she called Kai to say that the next-door neighbor was in the middle of a family barbecue and would not be able to accommodate the second horse.

Kai was undaunted. He called the next-door neighbor, introduced himself, and then proceeded to explain to this man why it was important that he get both horses to the house.

"You see," Kai explained, "we celebrate our anniversaries monthly, and this is our eleventh month. Well, naturally, I wanted to do the best I could for my wife. . . . You're married, aren't you?"

"Well, yes, I am. . . ."

"Well then, you can understand why it is so important to let your wife know just how much you love her, right?"

"Sure, right, right."

"So I thought that two horses and riding lessons would be the perfect anniversary gift. And if I don't get both horses, it won't be quite fair, will it?"

"I guess not. . . ."

"I know you're in the middle of a family barbecue, but could I invite you and your family—"

"Well, actually, it's my daughter and her husband and the grandchildren. . . ."

"Let me take this opportunity to invite you to come over with the horse and trailer, to meet my lovely bride. Do you ever watch the '700 Club'?"

"Oh, sure we do, most of the time."

"My wife is the co-host of the show, Danuta. And I'd like to invite you over to meet her. Bring your family as well."

"You know something, mister, I'm going to do just that. But not to meet her. I want to meet you! You're some kind of a guy!"

And with that, the dear man put away his chicken and the barbecue, took off his apron, loaded his family into the car, hitched up the trailer, picked up the horse, and drove to The Wild Kingdom—so he could meet a man who celebrated his love for his wife monthly.

It was a terrific surprise for me. I was in the kitchen when I saw two sprightly stepping Arabian horses prancing down the driveway. I closed my eyes and shook my head, hoping I was not hallucinating. Two and a half hours later the barbecue was back on, and the next-door neighbor of the horse lady had a story to tell his grandchildren.

Valentine's Day is always a special treat for lovers, and a great excuse to go all out. That particular year, the year of the horse, I came up with a brilliant idea. I was going to surprise Kai with breakfast in bed—catered! I found a catering service that didn't mind driving the forty-five minutes out to the country at five o'clock in the morning, which in itself was a miracle! I asked that they arrive dressed as a butler and maid, and that they arrive in secret! I unlocked the front door and left instructions that they prepare the five-course breakfast as quietly as possible, then knock on the bedroom door when ready to serve.

At half-past five, in the dark silence of the early morning, a knock on one's bedroom door sounds like a cannon going off. Kai jerked straight up in bed, the covers falling off his huddled shoulders. Adrenaline was pumping.

"What's that? Who's there?" He whispered.

"Come in!" I chanted merrily.

Kai swung around and looked at me as though I were insane, his eyes as wide open as they ever would be. The door swung open and a tuxedoed butler bearing coffee, roses, and the morning paper on a silver tray marched in as if he had been working for us for years.

"Good morning, sir! Good morning, madam! Breakfast will be served in a few minutes. Coffee?"

"Good morning, Raymond. Yes, coffee would be marvelous!" I gushed.

"For heaven's sake!" Kai laughed. "How wonderful!"

"Happy Valentine's Day, darling. I love you."

Breakfast included a pineapple boat loaded with fruit, terribly fattening eggs Benedict, homemade pastries, and chocolates, muffins, and strawberry crepes. A bit much, I'll admit, but after all, it *was* Valentine's Day!

Kai is one of the most romantic men I have ever known. His sensitivity, his sense of timing, drama, and enthusiasm for finding new ways to express his love is exceptional. On our eighteen-month wedding anniversary, Kai planned a serenade of our song, "Blue Moon." He chose that particular gift because a full moon would be blazing down upon us, and he wanted us to be in the moonlight for the occasion. It was 9:00 P.M. when Kai picked up his guitar, took me by the hand, and led me outside to the middle of the lawn.

"Look at that!" he said, as he threw his head back and looked at the sequins scattered across the night sky. "You know what some people say about the stars?" he whispered.

"What do some people say?" I whispered back, with my face tilted up to the moon glow.

"Some people say that the stars are actually holes in the floor of heaven."

I grew dizzy thinking of the millions of angels swirling across the heavens, tramping across the floor with the tiny holes in it. I strained my eyes to see a flash of an angel's wing, or the sweep of a robe, any movement behind the luster, drinking in the theme of God's footstool, our canopy.

Softly, in a murmur, Kai began to sing with his guitar, ". . . Blue Moon . . . you saw me standing alone. . . ." I gently withdrew from my reverie and smiled at the man I was so glad I had married. Suddenly, from the corner of my eye, I thought I saw something move in the dark. I turned sharply toward the vision I imagined. It was still there. Was it floating? It was moving! It was glowing, eerily white, something tall, coming closer. I gave out a startled cry! It was a ghost!

"Kai!" I managed to mutter. "Kai! It's a . . . it's a . . . man!"

It was a man, a man wearing a full white tuxedo, complete with tails, and a top hat. His white suit was glowing blue in the moon wash. As he came closer, I saw the bouquet of red and yellow roses in his arms.

When the "ghost" finally came close, he smiled and handed me the roses, then tipped his hat and said, "On behalf of the husband who loves you, happy eighteen-month anniversary!"

I was so pleased, and relieved, that I jumped up and kissed the man in the white tuxedo!

"Hey! What about me?" Kai smiled.

"You, Mr. Soderman, I'm going to thank privately."

Kai is not the only one who can completely bamboozle somebody. I did a pretty good job of that when I threw him a surprise birthday party. The invitation read:

> Please come to Kai's surprise birthday party.
> Saturday, April 12.
> (Boy, will he be surprised. His birthday is in August!)

One hundred people sneaked into the driveway and hid behind the barn, all of them carrying balloons. Doug Walker, a terrific drummer with a jazz band who also happens to work at CBN, ushered in his band and speakers. I had a catered barbecue all set up, without Kai's slightest suspicion that this was all for him.

He was under the impression that I was throwing a party for the youngest family member, Paul, who had just earned the MVP (Most Valuable Player) award in his soccer league. Kai did not investigate the commotion that morning, since I urged him to take advantage of the day and catch up on some work in the study.

All of a sudden I burst into the room. "Kai, come quick! A dog got one of our ducks!"

Kai jumped up from his desk and dashed outside with me. Standing in the woods to greet him were one hundred people and a jazz band, all singing "Happy Birthday to You." Obligingly, Kai began singing along, looking for the birthday person. When we got to "Happy Birthday, Dear Kai–i," he was still singing!

"What? My birthday? But, but . . . well, thank you so much!"

Kai felt that someone had made a big mistake, but he didn't want to hurt anyone's feelings, so he went along with the song until he realized it was a joke! Gag gifts abounded, including a Boy George makeup kit, kites, and jelly beans. The jazz band played and hamburgers disappeared. It was a grand time! Of all the birthdays Kai has had, his most memorable one was his *un*birthday.

Kai responded the following February with a surprise birthday party for me—at six o'clock in the morning! On a Wednesday! Forty people showed up with flowers, gifts and food, and there were telegrams from friends—all without my knowledge. I was busy getting ready for work and had no idea that downstairs I would be greeted with a chorus of "Surprise!"

But as I think back on all the surprises Kai has hit me with, there is one that stands out from all the rest. It all started with a sciatic nerve problem during fund-raising telethons. Because I am on my feet so long, the nerve begins to ache, and I need pressure applied to my feet and ankles and the backs of my knees, just to be able to sit for a few minutes at a time. Kai would try to relieve the pain the best he could, but the relief was always temporary.

One January, CBN decided to conduct half its fund-raising campaign from California. I went to Anaheim to take charge of the West Coast version of the telethon. Kai was in Virginia Beach, where he had a business of his own to run. Our thirty-second-month wedding anniversary occurred right in the middle of the telethon, but Kai did not forget. He sent thirty-two red and yellow roses to my hotel room in an enormous bouquet that resembled the flower displays in expensive hotel lobbies. It was a magnificent gesture to show that he loved me, and the card said he was flying in to Los Angeles that very evening.

One would think that would be gift enough, but that was only the beginning. During lunch that afternoon, a Federal Express package arrived with an unusual piece of paper in it. It was a certificate of some sort.

> This is to certify that Mr. Kai Soderman has successfully completed the Swedish Massage Training Course in Norfolk, Virginia, and is now a certified therapeutic masseur in Swedish massage.

What did this mean? Where did it come from? Was it some kind of a joke? I didn't understand, but I was intrigued. Later that evening, I drove to the airport to pick up Kai. Unknown to me, Kai had contacted the concierge of the hotel and had made certain "arrangements." When we opened the door of our hotel suite later that evening, I saw something I shall never forget.

Dozens of flickering candles were strategically placed around the room. And there, in the center of the room, like an altar, was a long, wide massage table, draped in a sheet and sprinkled with rose petals!

Kai grinned and swung me around in his arms, "Happy anniversary, honey!"

"What is it? What's happening?"

"For the last twelve weeks, I've secretly been taking Swedish massage lessons from a school in Norfolk. I figured that if my darling was in pain, I wanted to do something about it. I wanted to help heal you, and this was the best way I knew how."

"You mean *you* are a certified masseur!" I was flabbergasted. "My own personal husband, a masseur?"

"Your very own personal husband, a masseur. You want to try me out?"

One hasn't lived until one has lain on a bed of rose petals in candlelight, under the healing hands of a professional masseur-husband!

It is very difficult to speak about romance without sounding trite, or syrupy, or melodramatic, or a little crazy, unless it is happening to you, and then it is exciting, tingling, and adventurous!

On occasion, during speaking engagements, men have approached Kai. "Hey Soderman, we want to talk to you. Your romantic adventures are giving the rest of us fellas a bad name. Knock it off!"

"Hey!" Kai laughed. "That's not my problem, that's your problem!"

It is easy to overlook the expressions of love and to say they are "for young people only," or think they're too much trouble. In fact, sometimes people neglect that part of their love life, not because they want to but because they don't know how to light up the matrimonial fires after years of dim embers.

Imagination and creativity play a big part in expressing emotions. And the gesture does not have to be grandiose. It could be as simple as buying a funny card and tucking it in your loved one's jacket or purse. Or a mushy card that says "I love you" tucked under a pillow. Or a picnic dinner by candlelight on the living-room floor when the children have gone off to bed.

One couple I counseled complained that they had no love life, and didn't know how to find it after fourteen years of marriage and five children. The conversation was taking place during lunch, and I noticed that they didn't touch each other.

"You know," I said, "if Kai and I were sitting here, we would be holding hands and playing footsy under the table! Have the two of you ever thought of taking off alone, without the children, for a weekend? Maybe going to a quaint little hotel somewhere, tucked away at the beach, or the mountains? Just the two of you?"

They turned to each other and looked shocked at the suggestion. "What would we do there alone for an entire weekend?" she asked.

"Play a little footsy, and then let nature take its course!" I laughed.

Romance slips away slowly, imperceptibly, and over the years it is easy to forget the flames of love you once had for each other. Then love slips into mediocrity.

Sometimes people are afraid of taking the risk, of looking foolish, or being rejected, or wondering what your friends would say. There are dozens of excuses people have for not enjoying a fuller love life.

If anyone should have been afraid of taking the risk of looking foolish, it should have been Kai the day we were playing racquetball.

The score was tied at three games each. We were playing for the grand championship of the week. This last game was the tie breaker. The score was 20–19, my favor, my serve. Twenty-one was the winning point, and I was one stroke away from winning the championship.

Tension was high. We were drenched in perspiration and breathing hard. It had been a long series of games. I licked my lips. I was thirsty but I didn't want to break for water, not now. Not while I was just one point from winning the Kai-and-Danuta Grand Championship of the Week. Kai was in the backcourt, swaying back and forth, waiting for the serve. I bounced the tight blue ball on the floor, once, twice, three times, concentrating on the strategy of my next shot.

I'll shoot the corner and zing it in the left back corner, I thought. *His backhand is just weak enough that I could capitalize on it and take him by surprise.*

I bounced the ball again. I could smell victory in the lacquered wood of the court, and the harsh little *ping* sound of the ball that resembled the radar pings of a submarine. This was it. One more bounce . . . I turned slightly to glance back at him.

I screamed!

He was *mooning* me! He had dropped his pants, bent down, and blazed his two round cheeks at me, in full cinematic color! I missed the ball, blew the serve, and lost the game. And even though I claimed unfair advantage, Kai won by a rump.

Now that took guts! It was a risky thing to do. But what a memory. We still laugh about it. I suppose one of the reasons Kai took the risk of exposing himself, in more ways than one, was that he could trust me.

Now the only reason I'm telling this story is I'm trusting that although it's a little personal, you will understand just how important it is to have a sense of humor. A sense of humor is a requirement for romance. It adds a sparkle of spontaneity, and even adventure, to love.

And the good news is it's never too late to learn!

This is not to say that we have some exclusive claim to perfection. Far from it! We have our share of blowups, like the time we were ready to call it quits on a cruise to paradise. . . .

Chapter Eleven
Fighting Fair

We had never been on a cruise before, but we knew what to expect because we watched the television commercials. A cruise meant isolated beaches and food that stretched out for a hundred yards. A cruise meant romance, and more time with each other.

Lately, we ourselves had been like two ships passing in the night. We needed this vacation, and we would dangle it in front of each other as an encouragement during difficult times. The cruise was coming!

My schedule was demanding more and more of me. I flew to Detroit, then Chicago, and then took the red eye to Sacramento. I hadn't slept in thirty-six hours. I reached the fairgrounds in Sacramento, where a Christian exposition was in full swing. It was one of the hottest days of the year, with temperatures close to one hundred degrees. My body ached from traveling, and my eyes burned for sleep.

A crowd of people began to gather. Someone grabbed me by the arm and began to tug me in one direction, while someone else was pulling me in the opposite direction. Two or three others were asking for autographs. Suddenly I lost focus, and my knees buckled. I was fainting. Someone caught me and leaned me against a wall. A glass of water appeared and I was revived enough to finish the afternoon. But there was still the evening's obligations, an appearance at a small gathering of people in a home for a charitable organization.

I decided to grab a few hours' sleep in a hotel room. I pulled the curtains closed and sprawled out on the bed with the air conditioning pouring down on me. I began to tremble with exhaustion. I had to talk to Kai. The phone rang and his warm Swedish voice answered.

"Hello, Kai Soderman speaking."

"Kai? Oh, Kai!"

"Darling, are you okay?"

"Kai, just talk to me . . ." my voice quavered.

"Oh, my sweetheart, I love you!"

"Oh, Kai, it's so good to hear you! I miss you. I'm so tired. It's been such a long week . . . just talk to me."

"I want you to close your eyes. Are they closed?"

"Yes."

"And I want you to feel my arms wrapped around you, holding you close, and tight. I want you to feel God's arms around us both, keeping us safe."

"Mmmm," I sighed, "that feels good already."

"The Lord and I want you to know how much we both love you. Dear Jesus, keep my beloved close to You and refresh her in her work for You. Give her comfort and peace, holy Father.

And sweet Holy Spirit, settle Your strength upon her, and bring her home quickly and safely to me.''

"Thank you, Kai," I whispered into the phone.

"Darling? Remember, the cruise is coming!" Kai said cheerfully.

"The cruise is coming. Good night, sweetheart."

"Good night, my love."

It was springtime, and the cruise was coming in the fall. Fall seemed a long way off.

The worst drought in a century struck the Southeast the summer of 1986. The parched ground burned the corn crops, and farmers lost millions of dollars. The water tables and reservoirs reached dangerously low levels, and city councils initiated water-rationing programs. The sun drilled down relentlessly, day after day, making headlines across the country.

On The Wild Kingdom, the water started tasting funny. We read that seawater was seeping into the shallow freshwater tables. There wasn't enough fresh water to hold the seawater back. Grocery stores had a run on gallon-sized containers of spring water. Even our ducks welcomed a cool-down with the hose. My tomato plants shriveled up. We were shriveling up. Would summer never end? Would autumn never arrive? Was the cruise never coming?

We were in different cities the day of the cruise. I flew to Miami from San Diego, Kai flew from New York. We met each other at the airport. Kai looked haggard and pale from his four days in New York City. This cruise would fix everything. We hailed a taxi. There was no drought where we were going. No noise. No business meetings. No speaking engagements. No crowds. There would be sunshine and peace.

It hardly looked like a ship. It was more like a huge, white building, fifteen stories high, four football fields long, dotted with tiny symmetrical windows. It was one of the largest sailing vessels in the world. We were put out at the curb with our luggage huddled about us. A large group of men were sitting on crates nearby, laughing at a joke we didn't hear.

One of the men walked over to us, spied our luggage, and said, "You goin' on a cruise?"

He took our bags and pointed us to a doorway marked SECTION A AND B. At the end of a long hall, and a set of escalators, we emptied out into a large auditorium. At the entrance, a loud man was selling gaudy sunglasses "cheap, for you," he said. An irritated woman shoved some papers in our hands. "Fill out this form, over there." She motioned to an orange bench off to the side, without looking up at us.

We were finally directed to the gangway that led us onto the ship. If it didn't look like a ship on the outside, it hardly resembled a ship on the inside. We walked into a large pink-and-green lobby. A green tile fountain embedded with mosaic fish was in the middle of the floor. A fishnet hung from the side of the fountain, fastened with glued-on seashells. Red-and-green neon lights designated the purser's office, where one could find stamps, maps, information, and postcards.

We were directed to the veranda level for our room, located six flights up. As we climbed the staircase past the first level, neon lights flashed CASINO. Another level showed a couple dancing in neon animation. This was the Las Vegas of the high seas! A floating casino. The higher we climbed, the lower my heart sank. Some people ran down the stairs past us, laughing harshly, carrying tall plastic glasses filled with pink frothy liquid and little yellow paper umbrellas stuck into pieces of half-chewed orange slices.

"There must be a party going on somewhere," I said, smiling weakly at Kai.

On the veranda level we found our room, one of the finest

suites on board. It even had its own balcony. The room had a couch, a television set, and a small refrigerator. And twin beds.

"Don't worry," Kai said, "we'll be all right." He threw open his arms and we hugged.

"We haven't seen everything yet," I said optimistically.

I was right about that—we hadn't seen *anything* yet.

With four mighty blasts from its smokestacks, the ship began to move. I was hoping for dangly paper things that you throw to well-wishers on the dock, but the massive ship lumbered out of the harbor with little fanfare, and there were no dangly paper things, no well-wishers on the dock, only a parking lot and a barking dog.

"Well, we're off!" I said cheerfully. "Look out, vacation, here we come!" I pulled a few things from my carryon bag, including a book I had been promising myself to read one day, *The Gulag Archipelago* by Aleksandr Solzhenitsyn. I wondered why I had chosen such a dreary book about Soviet internment camps during Stalin's reign of terror, as vacation material. . . .

Neither of us had eaten since breakfast on the plane, and that was hours ago, so we called for room service.

"No ma'am, there will be no food served until after the emergency drill."

"Emergency drill? What emergency drill?"

"In about forty minutes there will be an emergency drill. You will be informed about it over the loudspeaker."

"Okay, fine. So how about a small basket of fruit or something? You see, we haven't eaten—"

"I'm sorry, ma'am, no food until—"

"Yes, I know, until after the emergency drill. But listen, how about a sandwich from one of the open grills on board?"

"Sorry, ma'am, we're not allowed to serve food until—"

"After the emergency drill. . . ." Now we both completed the sentence together.

The emergency drill went off without a hitch. Kai and I stood in the hot Miami sun looking like puffed-up tangerines in our bulky orange life vests. On every level, every passenger stood in single file, quietly sweating, waiting for orders to disassemble. We waited this way for more than half an hour. One elderly lady pulled out a chair and sat down.

"No ma'am, I'm sorry, no sitting," barked a blond drill sergeant.

Now, I'm all for emergency drills. I completely understand the need for emergency procedures. I had recently read an article on the *Titanic* in *National Geographic,* and I was fully appreciative of any and every attempt to get me off that floating hotel in one piece, should we hit a disoriented iceberg or plow into an island, or get burned out by terrorists. But at the time we were still in business suits, our luggage would not arrive from down below for another five hours, we were tired, we were hot, we were hungry, and we were standing like little orange soldiers in rows of four, watching eighteen-year-old boat directors flirting with one another. We needed to get on with the cruise, the food, and the relaxation.

Back in the room, I picked up the phone.

"Room service? We'd like two large hamburgers—"

"I'm sorry, ma'am, we don't serve hamburgers."

"Okay, how about a couple of bowls of hot soup and two tossed salads."

"No ma'am."

"No?"

"No ma'am, no hot food."

"Okay how about a club sandwich, with coffee—"

"Sorry, ma'am, we don't have club sandwiches."

"So what do you have?"

"We have an American cheese sandwich on white bread, peanut butter sandwich, or a bacon, lettuce, and tomato sandwich."

"Great! We'll have two BLTs and coffee."

"Sorry, ma'am, only cold drinks in cans."

"Ooookay . . . we'll have two BLTs and two Cokes."

When the BLTs arrived an hour and a half later, we were too hungry to notice that they were cold. The bacon was sticking to the top crust of the white bread by its refrigerated fat, and you could see through the tomato. There was no mayonnaise, no butter, no lettuce, and it was all wrapped in cellophane on a white paper plate. We figured it would hold us until dinner. A cozy little dinner for two, by candlelight, next to a window where we could watch the waves go by, would make up for a difficult start.

We sat at a table for eight, and met the group of people with whom we would be sharing our meals for the next seven days. Dinner was served in a bright, boisterous room, detonated with Happy Birthday songs every few minutes.

Dinner was frozen vegetables, baked potatoes, reconstituted turkey meat, beet-and-onion salad, and ice cream for dessert. I was looking forward to the lavish buffets to come. Tomorrow was bound to be better.

It wasn't. A sharp pain in Kai's back literally immobilized him. Walking in New York City for miles in cowboy boots with inch-and-a-half heels had thrown his back into spasm. The pain was so acute, he lay in bed all day and slept. That evening, he was still in too much pain to move, so instead of going to dinner, I called room service.

"Hello, room service?"

"Yes, this is room service," replied a Latin man with a very thick accent in a halting and uncertain voice.

"I need some dinner sent to our room, please. Do you have a menu?"

"A what you want?"

"A menu—do you have a list of food?"

"You want delivered room service?"

"Yes, that's it. What is for dinner?"

"You have a cheese sandwich, a peanut butter sandwich, or bacon and tomato sandwich."

"No, I need dinner, not sandwiches."

"No hot food."

"We'll take two BLTs and two Cokes."

That day and that night, as Kai slept, I watched both in-house movies, twice.

The next day the sun was intensely bright, the sky bluer than I have ever seen it. The ship cut through the water with astonishing grace, and flying fish danced in the crest of the waves. On the balcony, the wind smothered me with the warm smells of ocean and sky. This was going to be a great day!

It wasn't. Kai's back was no better. The only time it didn't hurt was when he was lying down. I fixed up some pillows on the chaise lounge and encouraged him to lie out in the sun on the balcony. Still, bed was more comfortable. We had missed breakfast, and we were missing lunch.

"Hello, room service? Is there any way we could get some hot food delivered to our cabin?"

"We have cheese sandwiches, peanut butter. . . ."

"We'll have two BLTs and two Cokes."

The remains of the previous night's BLTs sat in a small, soggy puddle in the middle of a paper plate. The new sandwiches sat next to it. They hadn't begun to thaw yet. Empty soft-drink cans and paper napkins littered the counter tops. We ate in silence. Kai went back to bed. I sat in the sun on the balcony, reading *The*

Gulag Archipelago. I was reading about the deprivation of food and sleep in the interrogation centers.

By dinner time, Kai was still not able to get up. I called room service.

"Room service? Listen, my husband is not feeling very well, and we have to have some hot food sent to the room."

"We don't serve hot—"

"Food," I said, finishing his sentence. "Yes, I know, but for the past two days, all we have eaten is bacon, lettuce, and tomato sandwiches, and we need some real food, from a real restaurant!"

"But we—"

"Could I speak to someone in charge?"

"In charge?"

"Yes, you know, the supervisor in charge of room service?"

"I get you the headwaiter."

"Hello?" A timid voice came over the phone.

"Hello, are you in charge?"

"Hello?" The voice asked again.

"Hello," I answered, "are you the supervisor in charge of room service?"

"Hello. Yes. I am food waiter."

"Would you please bring us a dinner menu, for hot food. My husband is not well, and we need some food brought to the room."

"He is sick?"

"Yes, he is sick."

Fifteen minutes later a waiter arrived to take our order. He could not speak a single word of English. I used hand signals to ask questions about the menu, and then wrote out the order for him on his pad.

Half an hour later, the waiter knocked on our door. "That was quick!'' I said, as I opened the door. But there was no food with him.

Through my broken Spanish and more hand signals, I learned he had given us yesterday's menu, and we had to repeat the entire procedure again. I wrote a new order on his pad. It had taken nearly three hours of negotiating and explaining, but real food finally came to cabin V-3. It was hot. It was on real plates. Nothing else mattered.

Kai's pain remained intense, sapping all his strength, and he drifted back to sleep for the night. I watched the in-house movies for the third time. I read my Bible. I stood on the balcony and studied the amazing Caribbean stars, bright as shattered diamonds. The ship was charging through the inky waters of the night.

By the morning of the third day, Kai and I again prayed for some relief from the pain. Relief did not come. By midday, and another round of bacon, lettuce, and tomato sandwiches, I was losing my patience with this pain, and so was Kai.

''Why don't you call on the ship's doctor and get some pain pills?'' I asked for the fourth time.

''Because it should go away soon by itself,'' Kai insisted.

''Kai, it's not going away. The only thing that's going away is our vacation. We have only four days left, and we haven't done anything!''

''So what do you want me to do about it? I can't help it if I'm in pain, Danuta.'' I knew he was getting annoyed with me by the way he used my name, but something had to be done.

''Just see the doctor, and get *out* of pain!'' I volleyed back.

''Okay, okay, okay!'' Kai got dressed and charged out of the room.

In the doctor's office Kai explained the problem and then added, ''And my wife is complaining because I'm not doing anything with her. This pain has kept me in bed for the last three days.''

"I don't blame her," replied the nurse and the doctor together.

It was an inflammation of the hip joint, and antiinflammation pills were prescribed for the pain.

Meanwhile the sun was setting in a brilliant display of orange sky and torn black clouds. I wished Kai could have shared it with me.

The pain pills helped a little bit. That night we went out to dinner and joined our six other friends at the table. Again, the food was only adequate, but it was hot, and we were free from the cabin. I still wondered about the buffets hundreds of feet long from the television commercials. I was looking forward to the lobster and the crab and the shrimp and the dazzle of culinary artistry.

"Where do you have the buffet?" I asked the waiter.

"Not today," he replied.

"I mean, the buffets, you know, out on the deck, for lunch and for dinner. . . ."

"We will have a midnight buffet tomorrow," he said.

"At midnight? You mean, after dinner? No, I don't mean midnight. I mean, where are the buffet meals *for* dinner?"

"No ma'am, only tomorrow night, at midnight, after people take pictures of it."

I wondered about that "taking pictures" bit. I figured people only take pictures of food if they don't see it every day. I didn't like the sound of it.

After dinner we walked along the deck, and ducked into one of the four lounges on board to see some of the nightlife. A man at a piano bar sang to his cigarette smoldering in an ashtray in front of him, while eight women perched around the bar, deliberately dressed for the unexpected, sipped their drinks and envied his cigarette.

In another lounge that promised dancing, five off-duty waiters huddled in the corner of the bar as earsplitting rock 'n' roll blared out of loudspeakers to an empty gallery.

But the casino was in full swing. Money changers and cocktail waitresses wandered through the crowd of people elbowing one another for positions at the blackjack tables. The slot machines were guarded by women hypnotically plugging in coins and pulling down levers. They played without emotion, reacting to neither winning nor losing, as though the machine were the end in itself, the capricious companion.

We walked back to the cabin. This was not what we expected, but neither of us wanted to admit it out loud. Kai was exhausted and fell into bed. The pain had taken all his reserves during the past three days. He was asleep before he hit the pillow.

I read *The Gulag Archipelago*.

The morning of the fourth day started out promising. Kai woke up without pain. We were going to have brunch out on the deck, by the pool. I had visions of the brunch buffet loaded down with mouth-watering temptations. Expectations were running high.

There was no buffet. Instead, there was an indoor walk-through where one could order a hot dog or a hamburger with fries. We plunked the hamburgers on our trays and walked outside to the pool area, where we ate with our trays delicately balancing on our knees, wrestling with the wind for ownership of the ketchup and mustard packets. But at least we were outdoors, together, in the sunshine.

I was only halfway through my lunch when Kai finished off his hamburger. "Do you want some more iced tea?" he asked, getting up with his tray.

"No, I'm fine."

"I'm going to get another glass of tea. I'll be right back."

I took my time with lunch, pushing my face into the sun and the wind, nibbling on my french fries. Ten minutes later I had finished eating, and I looked around for Kai. He was nowhere to be seen. I waited a few more minutes, then gathered up my tray and headed back indoors to put the tray on the counter and my empty cup in the trash. I wandered back outside. Still no Kai.

Funny, I thought. *It shouldn't take this long to get a glass of iced tea.*

I sat for a time on the edge of the pool, wishing Kai were with me, talking to me, laughing with me, walking with me, anything. It had been a long three days without him and I missed him.

Suddenly there was an announcement over the loudspeaker that the purser's office was accepting film for developing during the next fifteen minutes. I dashed down six flights of stairs, stood in line at the window, deposited the film, and then rushed back up six flights of stairs. I ran to the cabin, thinking Kai might be waiting for me there. He wasn't. I had started back to the lunch area of the pool when I spotted him sitting at a counter, sipping his iced tea.

"Where have you been?" I shouted at him, breathless from my run up the stairs. "I have been waiting for you for the last twenty minutes! I thought you said you were just going for some iced tea."

"I did go for some iced tea," he said, "but then I needed to go to the bathroom, so I went back to the cabin."

"You went back to the cabin to go to the bathroom?"

"Well, it wasn't that far, and I prefer our bathroom to the public bathroom, so that's what I did."

"It took you twenty minutes to go to the bathroom?" I persisted.

"No, Danuta, it did not take me twenty minutes to go to the bathroom. While I was in the cabin, I decided to change from my jeans to my shorts since it was so warm outside. Besides, what's the big deal? Why is it so important for you to complain about me?''

He was getting impatient with me, but I couldn't help feeling as if I had been waiting for him for three days now, and even twenty minutes seemed like an eternity to me, so I pressed on.

"Well, the big deal is that I had lunch alone, again. And I'm waiting for you, again, while you're off in your own little world. I'm still stuck here, waiting for you for twenty minutes, and I'm tried of waiting for you. I want to have some fun with you!''

"It wasn't twenty minutes. It was fifteen minutes at the most. You always exaggerate, Danuta.'' He started walking away from me, toward our cabin, and I followed.

"Kai, it was at least twenty minutes, because I had to run down to the purser's office and back, finish my lunch, put away my tray, and look everywhere for you, while you were going to the bathroom in the cabin and changing clothes. You might have told me. Besides, why should you go to the bathroom in the cabin when there's a perfectly good one down below where we were eating?''

"I'm sick and tired of your complaining, Danuta. That's all you've done on this trip. I don't see why I have to account to you for every little thing I do, and every second I spend.'' Kai slammed the door of the cabin.

"I haven't been complaining at all, Kai. How can you say that! I haven't seen you long enough to complain. You've been sleeping for the last three days!'' I shouted, feeling unjustly criticized. "You have taken me totally for granted throughout this entire time, while I've been nursing you and catering to all your needs. All you can think about is yourself!''

"I can't help it if I'm in pain!'' he hollered at me.

"You could have seen the doctor on the first day, instead of waiting through three days of a very expensive vacation!" I shouted back.

"I'm sick of it, Danuta. I'm sick of this and I'm sick of your criticizing me and constantly complaining. I'm sick of it! And I'm finished talking about it." He threw his briefcase on the bed and began going through his business papers, ignoring me and ignoring my side of the story.

"Listen to me!" I shouted. "Look up from those papers and listen to me!" He acted as if I weren't there. "I will not be ignored, and bullied, after what I've put up with for the last three days!" And with that, I tore his briefcase from his hand and hurled it across the room. It rolled up against the wall and fell on its side with a thump. I grabbed the papers remaining on the bed and threw them in the air. "You will listen to me! I don't deserve this from you!"

Kai stood up and pushed me away from the briefcase. I pushed him back. "Get out of my way," he growled.

"I will not get out of your way. I want you to spend some time with me!" I pushed him again.

He grabbed me by the arms, threw me down on the couch, and pressed his face up to mine. "Now listen. I've had all I'm going to take from you. I've had all I'm going to take! I'm through! I'm finished with you!" He shouted through gritted teeth.

He jerked himself off me, and I jumped up. "I hate you! I hate you!" I screamed at him. The tension between us had reached its zenith. Darkness flooded over us, and there was no light, no way out, no stopping the ugliness.

"Maybe I was never meant for marriage, Danuta. Maybe I just don't have it in me." Kai spoke too softly, too seriously. "I can't go on. . . ." He trailed off.

"Stop feeling sorry for yourself!" I rallied, hoping to shake him out of this dangerous slide to hopelessness.

"Leave me alone, Danuta. Just leave me alone."

"I'll leave you alone! Be alone, stay alone!" I grabbed my purse, stuffed a few things in my overnight bag, and stomped out of the room, slamming the door behind me. I walked with deliberate speed to the upper deck, and suddenly realized I was on a ship in the middle of the ocean. I couldn't go anywhere. I was stuck here.

It was raining. Everything was miserable. I slumped on a stool and cried. Rain was pouring down on my head and forming little rivulets from my hair onto my face, mixing with my tears. My shirt was sticking to my back. I was exhausted. I was wet and I was cold. But most of all, I was feeling lost and hopeless and helpless. I wanted so much for this to be a special time for us. I had built up such expectations. We needed this rest so badly!

"Oh God, oh, dear God, what is going on?" I cried. "Show me, Lord, what to do! I don't understand what is going on! What is happening to us?"

I had no choice. I hated to do it, but I had to go back to the cabin.

I opened the door, closed it behind me, and stood in the middle of the room, lost and cold and wet, and hurting.

"I had nowhere to go," I said.

Kai looked up from his newspaper with a steely cold look in his eyes. "Just look at you," he sneered. "Just take a look at yourself."

"Kai, I can't believe this is happening to us. Please don't let this happen." I sat on a chair opposite him.

"What are you talking about? What? What?" He snapped.

"Kai, I need you right now. I'm scared." He picked up the paper and continued to read it. "Kai, for the love of God, have mercy on me!" I began to weep.

"What do you want from me?" he said unsympathetically.

"I want a f-f-f-friend." I was sobbing, trying to catch my breath.

"Well then, go and find someone who will satisfy you. Go on! Go!" he growled back at me.

"I c-c-can't. I'm s-s-stuck on this boat, and I don't have a f-f-friend I c-c-can talk-talk to." My shoulders were jerking up and down and my diaphragm was in spasm. I couldn't breathe, I couldn't talk. I struggled for composure. Kai kept his eyes riveted on the newspaper.

"Kai. I need a friend. I need a friend I can talk to. If I wasn't on this awful boat, I could call a friend and talk. I could go to someone's house. But I'm stuck here with you." I began crying again.

"We were friends before we were married," Kai barked back. "Whatever happened to that, Danuta? You used to say I was your best friend." He stood up in disgust, moved to his twin bed, and lay down on it with some pain.

"That's right," I said. "You used to be my friend, and I used to be able to talk with you about anything. Right now you're all I've got. I don't want my husband, I can't talk to him. I don't want anything to do with him. But I need my friend. I'm hurting and I ache all over."

"Well then, come over here," he said gruffly. "I'll be your darn friend." He scooted over as far as possible on the narrow bed and offered me the space next to him. I slowly walked across the room, slouched over, wet, and runny-nosed, and lay next to him on the bed, burying my head in his chest so I wouldn't have to look at him and be reminded that he was my husband.

"So, what's the problem?" Kai said reticently.

"It's about my husband," I replied into his chest, in a muffled voice.

"What did the bum do to you?" Now he was sounding more like my friend.

"Well, he got so angry with me, and he wouldn't listen to my side of the story." Encouraged, I continued. "You see, I really missed him these past few days, and it's been building and building inside of me, and I didn't tell him how I was feeling. And so the first time we got to do something together, which was having lunch on deck, he left. And it seemed like a long time to me, and I was very sensitive to time by now. And then he got so angry with me that he didn't leave me a space inside of him where I could go and feel safe. He shut me out completely, and he acted as if he didn't care whether I lived or died. It scared me."

"I know Kai quite well," Kai said, "and that just doesn't sound like him at all. Do you suppose there's something else going on with him?"

"Well, I don't know. He doesn't talk much to me about what's bugging him. He pretty much keeps that to himself. So if there is something bothering him, I'm left in the dark."

"He sounds pretty useless to me," Kai answered. "Do you want me to dump the bum overboard?" Kai suddenly caught himself playing the part of my friend too well.

"Yeah," I said, squirming with delight, "throw the bum overboard for me."

We lay quietly on the bed in each other's arms for several silent minutes. And than Kai started to pray.

"Dear heavenly Father, in the name of Jesus I ask for Your forgiveness."

"Me too," I whispered, my face still buried in his chest.

"We have sinned against You and against each other. Forgive my anger and my hardheartedness toward my wife, dear Lord." He kissed the top of my damp head. "And in the name of Jesus, Satan, we rebuke your hand against us during this trip. We rebuke your presence in this room and aboard this ship! You spirit of corruption, we come against you, in Jesus' name. You have no authority here!''

I clung tightly to Kai. Something was happening. It was victory!

"Do you feel it?" Kai asked. "Do you feel it?"

The change was remarkable. I sat up and looked around the room as though seeing it for the first time. The sun was peeking through the clouds and shining crystalline through the window, spilling down upon us, stroking us with every dip and bow in the course of the ship on the waves. The heaviness was gone.

"Why didn't we pray sooner?" Kai asked.

"We have been under a heaviness ever since coming on this ship," I said. "It took us this far before we saw it."

"Never again," Kai vowed. "Never again will I allow this to happen."

We learned a valuable lesson that day. We learned how to fight fair.

To fight fair, we need to do four things. First, we have to give each other the opportunity to express our feelings. Second, in the midst of battle, there must be a special place in us for the other person to find a harbor of safety and trust. Third, we always need to remember that our love is too significant to amputate it with pride. And fourth, no matter what the circumstances, no matter what the problem, we always have a mediator in Jesus Christ.

And I learned one other thing: Kai Soderman is still my best friend.

Chapter Twelve
Our Spiritual Road Map

*T*his book is a road map. It is the spiritual blueprint of two lives. When we are in submission to God, we complete God's plan for us. And then through us, we help complete God's plan for others.

A perfect example of following a spiritual road map was the time Kai and I drove back to Warren, Vermont, the site of our honeymoon, to celebrate our second wedding anniversary. As we were packing to leave, Kai found a book on the floor of the closet. "Does this belong to you?" he asked me, showing me a book and four tapes entitled, *The Gifts of the Holy Spirit.*

"No," I said. "I've never seen it before."

"Do you want to keep it?" he asked.

"No, I don't think so," I said. "We have several books on the subject in the library."

"Good. Then let's take it with us." I thought that was rather unusual since neither of us wanted it. Why should we bring it along with us? But nothing more was said about the book, and we started off to enjoy our second honeymoon at nine o'clock that Saturday morning.

It was early October, and the thought of driving through the Vermont countryside at our favorite time of year sounded beautiful. Unfortunately, by the time we hit the New Jersey Turnpike, it was already dark, and we hadn't seen one autumn leaf yet. It was my turn at the wheel. We felt fairly confident of the road because we had taken this drive just a year before, although that time it was daylight.

Several hours had gone by when Kai, who was navigating, said, "This map is wrong."

"The map is wrong?" I said, looking at him sideways, with one eye still on the road. "What do you mean, the map is wrong?"

"It just doesn't seem right to me. But don't worry, I know how to get us there without the map."

He folded up the map and slipped it back in the glove compartment. I decided not to share my opinion about the map's being wrong. I would be the submissive wife and just drive, and leave the navigating to Kai.

Another half hour had gone by when Kai pointed to an exit sign along the highway and said, "That's it! Exit Twenty-two A. Turn off here."

I faintly remembered an Exit 22A, so we turned off the highway. We found ourselves on an isolated, dark country road, and crept along for almost an hour before we crossed an old wooden bridge.

"Hey, you remember that bridge!" Kai said with a grin.

"Yeah!" I said with enthusiasm.

Then we passed a little white church set back from the road.

"Hey! Do you remember that church?" Kai said, smiling and pointing.

"Yeah!" I said, feeling more and more encouraged that soon we would be in front of that fireplace in our little cabin in the woods.

An hour and a half later we crossed over that wooden bridge again. The third time we crossed the bridge Kai said in a growl, "Do you remember that bridge? Do you see that church?"

"Yeah. I remember," I grumbled.

It was now past midnight. We had expected the trip to take eleven hours. We had now been driving for more than fifteen hours. And it was obvious we were lost.

"Lord Jesus," Kai prayed, "help us find our way."

Just then, flashing in the headlights was a tiny sign we had not seen the previous two trips around. It was the size of a yardstick, stuck in the embankment alongside the road. In black vertical letters on a white background it read, WARREN.

"Yippee!" we cheered. We were not lost after all. "Thank You, Lord!"

"Obviously, we are just missing a turn somewhere," Kai said hopefully. "Let's just keep our eyes peeled. Warren can't be too far away."

We brightened up, thinking of how close we were to the ski resort and the cabin, and that fireplace in the woods. We slowed down to look at huge trees looming over the road, heavy with full branches, trying to make out what color the leaves were in the dark.

"Oh, boy! I bet that tree is beautiful, if we could see it!" I said, slowing down to a crawl and flashing the full-beam head-lights at it. We had been waiting all year to see Vermont in the fall again, and even though it was 1:45 A.M., we were still anxious to see the foliage, even if everything did look as if it had come out of an inkwell.

Thinking we remembered a small road that intersected the "loop" we were on, we turned on to it and drove past a dark field on our left, where two cows stood stoically in the spillover light of the headlights, looking like cutouts from a Georges Seurat painting. Even they were sleeping. There was no gas station, no 7-11, no McDonald's where we could ask for directions. We were going by feel. And it was feeling all wrong.

Suddenly, up ahead, we saw one little light shining. Like moths to a flame, we zeroed in on the light. It was our first sign of humanity in over four hours. As we drove closer, we realized it was coming from the second story of a house, and there, in the window, was the profile of a man. He appeared to be reading.

I parked the car and Kai jumped out. "I sure am glad someone else is up at this unholy hour." He slammed the door and walked across the gravel toward the front door, but there were huge cinder blocks from a construction project in his way, and it was too dark to get around them. So Kai scooted around the corner, looking for another entrance.

He couldn't find another entrance, but what he did find was a ladder, leaning up against the side of the house. So Kai climbed the ladder to the window. Reaching out as far as he could from the ladder, he knocked on the second-story window. The profile of the man in the window jerked up, and he looked at the ceiling.

Knock-knock. Kai tried again to get the man's attention at the window. The profile snapped left and right and looked back up at the ceiling again. I can only imagine he must have been thinking he had enormous rats in the attic.

Kai tapped on the window a third time. "Excuse me!" he called out in his lilting Swedish accent. "Excuse me!" He was waving now at the profile that finally came full-face, frozen, toward his second-story window.

The man opened the window and stuck his head out. "Can I help you?" he said, somewhat amazed.

"Oh, yes, thank you," Kai said, hanging on to the ladder with one hand and the window ledge with the other. "You see, we seem to be lost."

"I can see that," said the man in the window.

"And we were wondering if you could tell us where Sugar Bush Inn is," Kai continued.

Since Kai offered no explanation about why he was hanging off a two-story window at 2:30 A.M., the man in the window did not inquire. Instead, he ducked his head inside and called to his wife, "Hey, honey! Do you know where Sugar Bush Inn is?"

His wife didn't know.

"Sorry, mister. I don't think we've ever heard of the place. Are you sure you have the right town?"

"I'm sure we do. This is Warren, right? And Sugar Bush Inn is one of the largest ski resorts around. You know, where all the tourists go skiing. . . . It's the biggest attraction in all of Warren, Vermont!"

"This is Warren, all right," the man in the window said. "Warren, New Hampshire."

"New Hampshire!" Kai repeated. "This isn't Vermont?" He couldn't believe his ears.

"Listen, why don't you folks come in and have some coffee, and we'll show you a map." And with that, the man in the window disappeared. Kai climbed down from the ladder and walked toward the car with the lowest hangdog expression I have ever seen on the face of a man.

Once inside the house, we were greeted warmly by Bill and Alice. As we made our way across the living room, suddenly we heard a choir of angels singing. Now it was our turn to jerk our heads up to the ceiling and side to side. The music was coming from the stereo. It was a tape of the "Hallelujah Chorus."

"Hey," Kai said, "that's beautiful music. Do you folks listen to that kind of music a lot?"

"Yep," said Bill.

"Well, how about that!" Kai said cheerfully, fully expecting Bill to elaborate, but he didn't.

"So, are you folks Christians?" Kai was trying to engage this New Englander in conversation.

"Yep," Bill said.

"Well, how about that!" Kai repeated himself, looking at me with a wide smile on his face. "So are we!"

"Good," Bill said.

"Say, do you folks, by any chance, ever watch the '700 Club'?" Kai was really getting a charge out of all of this.

"Nope," said Bill.

"Oh, well, if you did, you'd see my lovely wife on television. She's the co-host of the show with Pat Robertson and Ben Kinchlow. And they talk about the Lord Jesus."

"Don't get cable," Bill said.

"Well, how about that . . ." Kai drifted off.

"So how did we end up in Warren, New Hampshire?" I asked, leaning over the map on the table.

"Well, it seems to me that where you want to go is here," Bill pointed, "and where you are is here."

"How far away from Warren, Vermont, are we?"

"Oh, I'd say at least four hours."

"Four hours!" we groaned, and looked at the clock. It was 3:00 A.M.

Bill and Alice invited us to stay in their guest room, but we figured since we had come this far, we might as well push it all the way to Vermont. I sipped a second cup of coffee and won-dered aloud why these dear people were up so late at night.

"We are waiting for a telephone call from our daughter in Germany," Alice explained. "Normally we would have been in bed hours ago."

Alice gave us a thermos full of coffee and Bill gave us a map that was "right." As we walked toward the door, Kai suddenly felt led to ask if we could all pray together.

"Do you mind?" he asked.

"No, not at all. We sure could use it," Bill answered.

We took one another's hands and bowed our heads. Just as Kai began to pray, he stopped and looked up at Bill.

"Is there something we need to pray for you?" Kai asked him.

"Well, we sure could use whatever prayers you've got," Bill replied.

"For anything in particular, Bill?" I asked.

"Well, I guess I can tell you. You see, in a couple of days Alice and I are going to have a prayer meeting in this house. It's going to be the first prayer group ever in Warren. And to tell you the truth, I've never held a prayer meeting in my life. Frankly, I don't know what to do or what to say. I guess I'm nervous about it." Bill bit the corner of his bottom lip, as though he thought he had said too much.

"Bill!" I brightened up. "You don't have to do anything! You don't have to say anything! Why don't you just let the Holy Spirit say it for you?"

"The Holy Spirit?" Bill said, glancing quickly at his wife.

"You really hit on something there," Alice said. "We've been praying for the gifts of the Holy Spirit for a long time. In fact, we were praying about that very thing just this evening."

You could have knocked us over with a feather. Kai looked at

me, I looked at Kai. "Bill, Alice, your prayers are answered!"
I said triumphantly.

The four of us praised and worshiped God for the next fifteen
minutes, and when Kai and I began speaking in tongues, Bill and
Alice whispered in tongues together. At half-past three in the
morning, they received the Baptism of the Holy Spirit!

Kai jumped up. "Oh, God!" he cried, and rushed out the
door. He returned with the book he had found on the closet floor,
the book neither of us wanted, the book he took along anyhow,
the book entitled, *The Gifts of the Holy Spirit.*

"Here," he said. "This is for you."

Bill walked us to our car with tears in his eyes. "I can't thank
you enough," he said.

"It wasn't us," Kai said. "It was the Holy Spirit. Danuta and
I always pray that God will make us His instruments. Tonight,
He answered that prayer."

We drove off into the darkness of the countryside, filled with
the light of the living God. Our hearts were beating like tiny
drums, and our spirits were revived. What were the chances, we
thought, of getting lost, driving to the right town in the wrong
state at the right time to deliver a book to two Christians in the
middle of the night—the only people with a light in the window—who had been praying for a blessing from the Holy Spirit?

Bill and Alice must have thought we were two very strange
angels. Angels or not, we were definitely messengers who got
lost for all the right reasons. We shall never forget that night
because it always reminds us that even when we're lost, we're
going in the right direction.

Our two lives had been like that trip in the night: a fast, furious
drive through the darkness looking for a destination that seemed
to elude us. Until we found a light in a window, a ladder against

a wall, and someone inside waiting for us . . . because God had us in mind for each other.

Perhaps your life seems the same. I don't know what you long for or what lies in store for you, but I know this: If you seek God with a passion, no matter what dark road you are on, there will be a lighted window for you, a ladder against the wall, and inside, Someone waiting.

When we look back at the past, we see now what we could not have seen then. Now, we see God's plan. Then we saw only swirling confusion, mistaken cues, despair, and human foible. But viewed retrospectively, we see a tapestry of perfection, a road map with a distinct and definitive journey through fields of wilderness, exploration, discovery, learning, and growth.

Our lives apart and our lives together have been formed along a path we could not have charted for ourselves. We did not have the vision for it. We were not big enough. This revelation has helped with our limited understanding of the present, and our absolute trust in God for our future.

Look with us at the past, with the eyes of God.

Kai found Harald Bredesen, after years of searching, and found the power of a personal Savior. Five days later Kai met me. He was the first person I told of my intuitive feelings that one day I would be used in a special way to encourage peace upon earth, and Kai, for some strange reason, felt a great conviction to support and respect that dream.

Five years later, Kai introduced me to Harald Bredesen, and Harald introduced me to my Lord and Savior, Jesus Christ. A meeting with the prime minister of Israel revealed to me a vision of a magnitude I only dreamed about, that one day I would be communicating with leaders of nations. During the next two years there was significant growth in my knowledge of the ways of

God. Visions of my ministry came to Jewish dreamers who never dream, and within two years I was working for CBN, interviewing the leaders of nations in the name of Jesus Christ.

Kai began by grappling with the meaning and purpose of his life as others saw it for him, but not as God sees it for him. When despair had taken him to the length of a cheap piece of rope, two bird-watchers made him pause to think of his children and the words of his oldest son, preventing his suicide. Searching for comfort in a second marriage spelled disaster until a spiritual hunger compelled him to go to Los Angeles to find Harald Bredesen, and the love of Christ Jesus. It was in Him that Kai found a purpose for his life. And that purpose spilled over to me. But it took us years of wilderness training, searching for God, and then growing in Him, before we could be complete for each other. We were on the periphery of each other's life. But that fused in us a deep foundation of friendship, and a deeper foundation of love.

I think of "wilderness training" when I think of the Israelites wandering in the desert for forty years, looking for paradise. Often there is a wilderness between us and the promised land. The path can take you through despair and futility if you are without God, but with God, there is an extraordinary rendezvous with hope. The Word says it best in 1 Peter 5:10:

> But the God of all grace, who hath called us unto his eternal glory by Christ Jesus, after that ye have suffered a while, make you perfect, stablish, strengthen, settle you.

And then there was the marriage proposal. Harald counseled Kai that when times are rough, make things as difficult for God and as easy on yourself as possible. In other words, give all worry and concern over to God. Read 1 Peter 5:6, 7:

> Humble yourselves therefore under the mighty hand of
> God, that he may exalt you in due time: Casting all your
> care upon him; for he careth for you.

To pray that I would propose was the easiest way for Kai to cast upon God his burden of love for me. God honored Kai's obedience in a strange way, through a prayer of mine involving wind chimes. Just as Kai wanted a sign that God would handle everything, I, too, prayed for a sign that God wanted me to marry Kai. The wind chimes rang, not when I *wanted* them to, but when God knew I would listen; after it was first resolved in my heart that I was in love with Kai. I have often wondered why the chimes didn't ring the night I asked for the sign. Would God want me to marry Kai only out of obedience, without first having love? The seed of love was planted first, and then the wind chimes confirmed my heart.

Kai knew we would be married. The peace of God gave him that knowledge. Colossians 3:15 tells us, "And let the peace of God rule in your hearts. . . ." To Kai that meant not having a mind of his own in the matter, but letting peace rule in his heart as an umpire.

Some people have questioned the right of Kai to marry for yet a third, and I might add, a final time. Kai did not have Christ in his life during his previous marriages, and I would assume that had he known Jesus, his first marriage would not have failed, nor, for that matter, would his second. Because Kai would have been different, his marriage would have been different. He would have reacted to problems with God's guidance rather than relying on himself. If we rely only upon our own judgment, our own self-imposed standards of morality, our own self-help programs, we will find only failure, because there is no perfection in us.

Had Kai belonged to Christ during those difficult times, he would have known of the power of prayer. He would have been able to seek the Word of God and find out how to handle his problems. If Kai had had the kind of prayer group we have today, a group of gentle, honest believers in whom the corporate body of Christ is used to minister to one another's needs with counseling, support, and prayer, he would have found meaning in the love of God and the sacrifice of His Son. The disappointments of life would not have been so profound, and his trust in God could have changed his situation completely.

But God never gives up on us. He found Kai, dusted him off, and set him on a course that would put away the old man and bring in a new creature.

> Therefore if any man be in Christ, he is a new creature: old things are passed away; behold, all things are become new.
>
> 2 Corinthians 5:17

As for me, I was looking for Mr. Right in all the wrong places, and all the time lying to myself. I wanted to be married, but I was afraid to admit it, afraid that unconditional love from a man would never happen for me, and so, to save myself from that harsh reality, I lied to myself, denying the need was there. But at the same time, I was not pining away.

A woman who is waiting to be married before she can realize her full potential is a lady in wasting. Too many times I hear the lament, "If only I had a husband, then I would be happy, and complete, and I could enjoy life." If you are miserable and incomplete *without* a husband, you will be miserable and incomplete *with* a husband! Your life will not find completion in the unity of two imperfect souls. The only unity and fulfillment comes from God Himself. Only God is faithful, and perfect, and He is the One we can throw our full weight upon and have no fear that He will buckle under the load.

And that is the biggest difference in a marriage based on Jesus Christ. When we hold Christ up higher than ourselves, as arbiter, mediator, and counselor, a tremendous burden is lifted from us because we don't have to find courage, strength, or wisdom within ourselves or within our own experiences. We find that in Him. And when we pray, He is there with us. We feel Him. We sense Him. We breathe Him in. When Kai and I pray together we experience the privacy of lovers in the unity of our spirits. To be unified in body, mind, and spirit in a marriage is to experience the greatest intimacy of all. It is the melding of two people in God Himself.

And there is something else that happens when God is the third partner in a marriage. Without Christ, pride is all one has. But with Christ, pride must be put aside. Sometimes we pray "white knuckle" prayers. When neither of us wants to, through fisted hands and clenched teeth, we put our differences before God and submit to Him, confessing our sins out loud before Him and before each other. Within a few minutes, the fisted white knuckles turn upward, and worship begins where the struggle ends.

918 – 9/11/84

My Dearest –

I need to record this moment in time to tell you of the overwhelming feeling of love and deep contentment you have placed in my heart. I think I would choose to die than to miss even a moment of the sweet happiness I hold inside because of you. You have richly increased my sense of identity, my place in this world, and the excitement of the path we both travel. I don't that I realized what emptiness was until I was filled with you.

I look to the years ahead with expectation of mischievousness, and the pursuit of excellence coupled with a sense of adventure, and surprise.

You make me love.
You make me laugh.
Hold me when I cry.
You are a fellow dreamer.
Half your soul is mine
And half my pillow, yours.
I love you beyond possibilities.
My husband, my gift, my jo—
My gossamer man,
I welcome you with open a—

Forever.

Danuta

Hello Darling,
Proverbs 18:22. Hip!
Hip! Hooray! Hallelujah!
Kai

"What are you doing the rest of your life? North and south and east and west of your life. I have only one request of your life – that you spend it all with me."
With all my love,
Kai

For 30 months of Joyous Love
Commitment to Excellence
Challenges of the Future
I thank you,
My Love is
Unending,
Kai

TO GOD'S
"BLOOMING" STA—
FROM HI—
AND
HUSBAND SUDOS!